HOW THINGS WORK
OCEANS

Other publications:

AMERICAN COUNTRY

VOYAGE THROUGH THE UNIVERSE

THE THIRD REICH

THE TIME-LIFE GARDENER'S GUIDE

MYSTERIES OF THE UNKNOWN

TIME FRAME

FIX IT YOURSELF

FITNESS, HEALTH & NUTRITION

SUCCESSFUL PARENTING

HEALTHY HOME COOKING

UNDERSTANDING COMPUTERS

LIBRARY OF NATIONS

THE ENCHANTED WORLD

THE KODAK LIBRARY OF CREATIVE PHOTOGRAPHY

GREAT MEALS IN MINUTES

THE CIVIL WAR

PLANET EARTH

COLLECTOR'S LIBRARY OF THE CIVIL WAR

THE EPIC OF FLIGHT

THE GOOD COOK

WORLD WAR II

HOME REPAIR AND IMPROVEMENT

THE OLD WEST

COVER

*Tethered to a ship on the ocean's surface, a diver
descends into the abyss in a Jim Suit, which can
withstand the pressure of water 2,000 feet deep.*

HOW THINGS WORK

OCEANS

TIME-LIFE BOOKS

ALEXANDRIA, VIRGINIA

Library of Congress Cataloging-in-Publication Data

Oceans
        p.   cm.   – (How things work)
    Includes index.
    ISBN 0-8094-7906-0 (trade)
    ISBN 0-8094-7907-9 (lib.)
    1. Ocean
    I. Time-Life Books.   II. Series.
    GC21.O27   1991
    551.46—dc20   91-15523
                                    CIP

How Things Work was produced by
ST. REMY PRESS

PRESIDENT	Pierre Léveillé
PUBLISHER	Kenneth Winchester

Staff for *OCEANS*

Editor	Pierre Home-Douglas
Art Director	Philippe Arnoldi
Assistant Editor	Christopher Little
Contributing Editor	George Daniels
Picture Editor	Chris Jackson
Designers	Chantal Bilodeau, Luc Germain
Illustrators	Maryse Doray, Nicolas Moumouris, Robert Paquet, Maryo Proulx
Index	Christine M. Jacobs

Staff for *HOW THINGS WORK*

Series Editor	Carolyn Jackson
Senior Art Director	Diane Denoncourt
Senior Editor	Elizabeth Cameron
Researcher	Nyla Ahmad
Administrator	Natalie Watanabe
Production Manager	Michelle Turbide
Coordinator	Dominique Gagné
Systems Coordinator	Jean-Luc Roy

Time-Life Books Inc. is a wholly owned subsidiary of
THE TIME INC. BOOK COMPANY

President and Chief	Kelso F. Sutton
President, Time Inc. Books Direct	Christopher T. Linen

TIME-LIFE BOOKS INC.

Managing Editor	Thomas H. Flaherty
Director of Editorial Resources	Elise D. Ritter-Clough
Director of Photography and Research	John Conrad Weiser
Editorial Board	Dale Brown, Roberta Conlan, Laura Foreman, Lee Hassig, Jim Hicks, Blaine Marshall, Rita Mullin, Henry Woodhead
PUBLISHER	Joseph J. Ward
Associate Publisher	Trevor Lunn
Editorial Director	Donia Steele
Marketing Director	Regina Hall
Director of Design	Louis Klein
Supervisor of Quality Control	James King

Editorial Operations

Production	Celia Beattie
Library	Louise D. Forstall
Correspondents	Elisabeth Kraemer-Singh (Bonn); Christina Lieberman (New York); Maria Vincenza Aloisi (Paris); Ann Natanson (Rome).

THE WRITERS

Fred Golden is a former senior writer at *Time* and assistant managing editor of *Discover*. In 1988-1989 he served as acting editor of *Oceanus* magazine.

Stephen Hart has written previously for the *How Things Work* and *Voyage Through the Universe* series. A resident of Port Angeles, Washington, he specializes in science and technology writing.

Gina Maranto is an award-winning science journalist who has written for *Discover*, *The New York Times Book Review* and numerous other publications.

Bryce Walker is a former writer and editor of Time-Life Books. He now works as a freelance writer, specializing in science, travel and history.

THE CONSULTANTS

Martin Bowen has spent 11 years building and operating unmanned submersible vehicles. He has also logged two months "flying" deep submergence robots from surface vessels.

Arnold Gordon, Professor and Head of the Physical Oceanography Department at Columbia University's Lamont-Doherty Geological Observatory, is a fellow of the American Geophysical Union and President-elect of the Oceanography Society.

Ken MacDonald is Professor of Marine Geophysics at the University of California at Santa Barbara. His specialty is the tectonics of mid-ocean ridges using manned submersibles, swath-mapping tools and measurements of Earth's potential field.

John Orcutt is a Director of the Institute of Geophysics and Planetary Physics at Scripps Institution of Oceanography. He has pioneered research on the structure of the oceanic lithosphere and rise axes.

David Ross is a Senior Scientist in the Department of Geology and Geophysics and the Sea Grant coordinator at Woods Hole Oceanographic Institution.

John Teal is a Senior Scientist in the Department of Biology at Woods Hole Oceanographic Institution.

For information about any Time-Life book,
please write:
Reader Information
Time-Life Customer Service
P.O. Box C-32068
Richmond, Virginia
23261-2068

CONTENTS

A clownfish swims among the tentacles of a sea anemone.

Waves can travel thousands of miles before reaching shore.

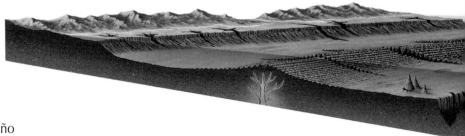

The ocean floor boasts one of the most diverse landscapes on the planet.

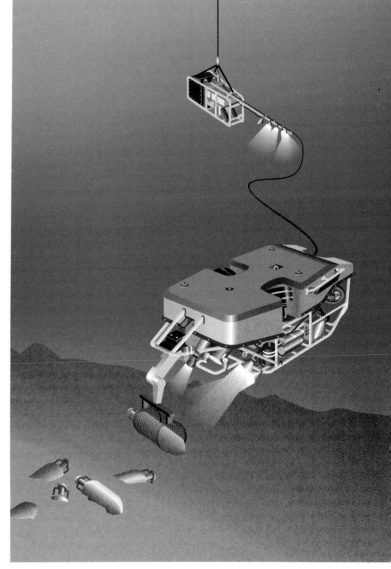

The remotely operated vehicle *Jason* retrieves relics from an ancient shipwreck.

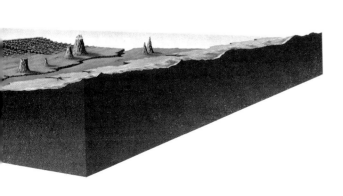

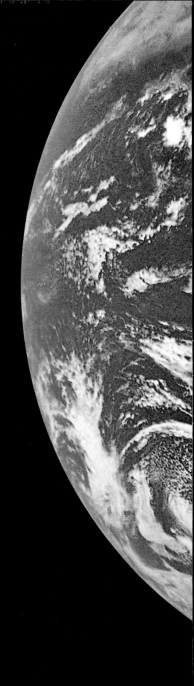

The Blue Planet

Call it Oceana. Covered with a briny mantle of water that blankets more than two-thirds of its surface, this planet clearly is misnamed Earth. Seen against the inky darkness of space, it is primarily a world of water. The magic liquid not only gives Earth its distinctive gem-blue color; it also has natured and nurtured life throughout most of the planet's four-billion-year history.

Some of the Sun's progeny—Venus and Mercury, for instance—suffer from metal-melting heat; others, such as Neptune and Pluto, are locked in a permanent ice age, with surface temperatures that hover near the -459°F of Absolute Zero. But the blue planet, 93 million miles from the Sun, is blessed with temperate conditions that, when combined with the unique chemical properties of the

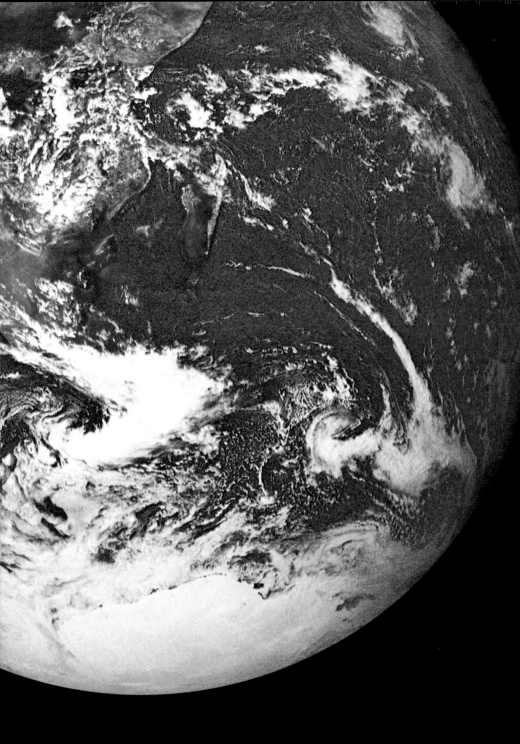

water molecule, result in a world where water exists in a liquid state. No other planet in the Solar System nor—as far as scientists have been able to discern—any other body in the universe possesses so benign a set of circumstances.

Water and the oceans make Earth unique. They make this planet, afloat in the sterile void of space, an oasis of life.

Photographed from the Apollo 17 spacecraft during the final Apollo mission to the Moon, the Earth vividly belies its name. The planet is mostly a watery realm.

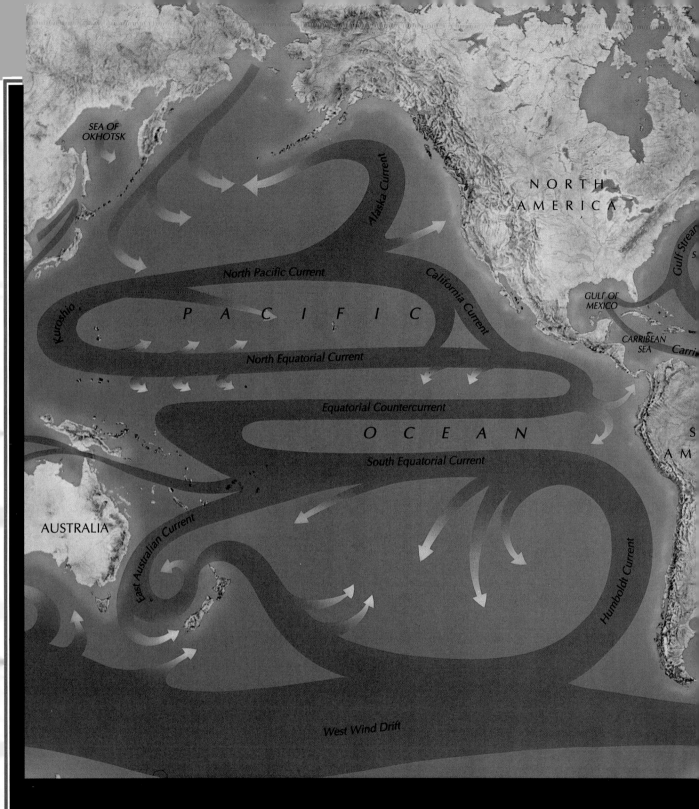

SEA OF
OKHOTSK

NORTH
AMERICA

Alaska Current

North Pacific Current

California Current

Kuroshio

P A C I F I C

Gulf Stream

GULF OF
MEXICO

North Equatorial Current

CARRIBEAN
SEA

Carri

Equatorial Countercurrent

O C E A N

S

South Equatorial Current

A M

AUSTRALIA

East Australian Current

Humboldt Current

West Wind Drift

The World's Oceans

From the days of earliest civilization, the oceans have challenged people to define and understand them. The ancient Greeks imagined that the oceans were an immense river encircling the Earth, and among their gods, Oceanus was second in might only to Zeus. Later, the Mohammedans spoke of the Seven Seas—the Mediterranean,

the East African Sea, the West African Sea, the China Sea, the Persian Gulf and the Indian Ocean. Today, oceanographers divide the world's oceans into three principal bodies: the Atlantic, the Pacific and the Indian.

Together, the oceans contain more than 300 million cubic miles of water. If the Earth were perfectly smooth, the ocean would cov-

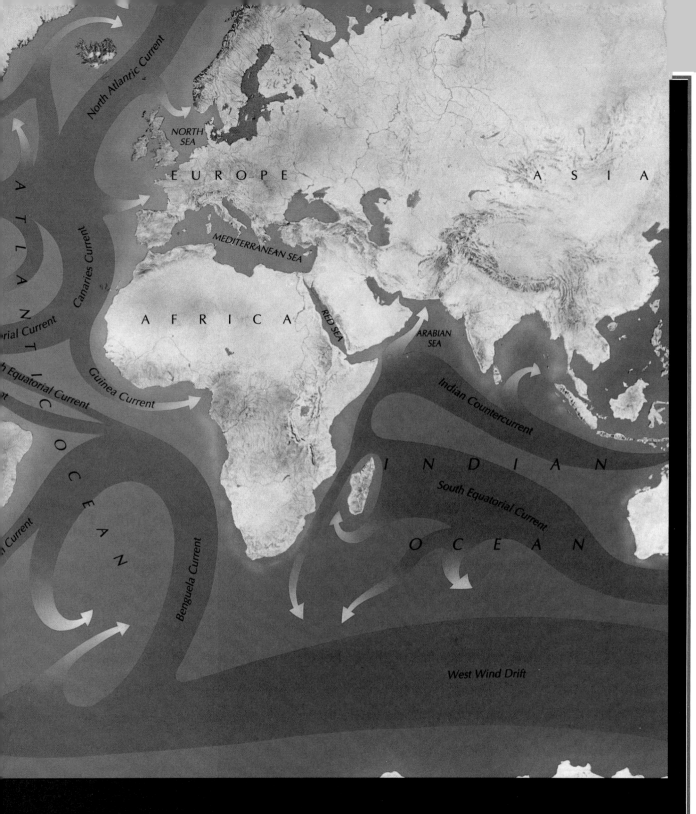

er it to a depth of 12,000 feet. The water that fills the immense ocean basins—which plunge as deep as seven miles in the Mariana Trench in the western Pacific—traces its origin to the early history of the Earth.

As the primordial planet was wracked by intense internal geological activity, water made its terrestrial debut, vented by fiery vol-

canoes that broke through the Earth's crust. Emerging into the coldness of space, the vapor was trapped by the Earth's developing atmosphere. Finally, the planet cooled enough for the vapor to condense and fall, under the force of gravity, into the first of the world's ocean basins more than three billion years ago.

Although the oceans carry different names, there is—as this illustration illustrates vividly—only one interconnected waterway in which the continents exist as islands, not barriers. The global sea is stirred by a worldwide pattern of winds that drive surface currents from the Arctic to the Antarctic.

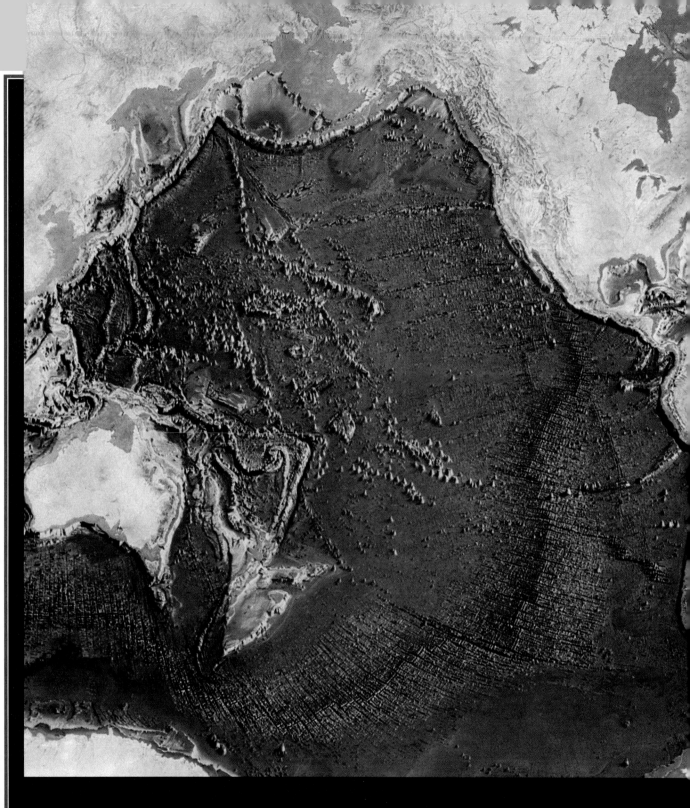

Seascape

"That which is far off and exceeding deep, who can find it out?" The question, posed in *Ecclesiastes*, summarizes the challenge that faced early oceanographers. The landscape under the ocean's waves was long *terra incognita*, obscured by an impenetrable blanket of water often miles deep. It was only in the 20th Century, when scientists learned how to bounce sound signals off the ocean floor and record their return time, that a picture began to emerge of that largely uncharted world.

Stripped of its water, the ocean reveals a topography as dramatic and diverse as any continental landscape, belying early beliefs that it was a monotonous terrain. Vast plains,

twisting canyons that stretch for hundreds of miles and fields of strange-looking mounds of solidified molten rock known as pillow lava—this is a setting that would not look out of place on a foreign planet. Dominating the surreal seascape is a 40,000-mile-long series of ridges six to 10 thousand feet high that winds its way through all the ocean basins.

Called the Mid-Ocean Ridge, it is the world's longest mountain range.

While spacecraft have skimmed by planets billions of miles distant and sent back thousands of vivid images of those distant worlds, the Earth's own ocean floor still remains imprecisely explored and its watery veil—for all mankind's efforts—only partially pierced.

When this astonishing map appeared in 1977, it presented the first comprehensive view of the Mid-Ocean Ridge, a mountain range that dwarfs anything found on land. It took oceanographers Marie Tharp and Bruce Heezen more than a decade to compile the map, using 100 years' worth of data.

THE RESTLESS OCEANS

When astronauts aboard the Apollo space missions first viewed Earth from afar, they marveled at the sparkling blue and white planet. Compared with the blackness of space, or the cratered, dusty lunar surface, it stood out as a warm and inviting world, the most hospitable in the Solar System. As they knew, and could plainly see, Earth's uniqueness lies in its large amounts of water, without which it would be as bleak and lifeless as the Moon.

The bulk of Earth's water—97.9 percent—is stored in its oceans, the great briny blanket vented from the planet's interior in the first half billion years of a 4.5-billion-year terrestrial history. Vapors, expelled from the primeval Earth as volcanic gases, condensed and fell as rain, filling up the planet's basins. Even today trace amounts of new, or "juvenile," water are being released from Earth's deep interior at the tectonically active mid-ocean ridges, where new sea floor is being created by the upwelling of lava, and by volcanoes on continental margins such as the "Ring of Fire" bordering the Pacific.

The oceans cover 71 percent of Earth's surface. Long before living things appeared on land, the first single-celled creatures arose in the seas. In all likelihood, water was the birthplace of life.

As long ago as the 16th Century, Leonardo da Vinci realized that "water is the driver of nature." But only now is mankind beginning to recognize how fully dependent all life is on the seas. In interaction with the atmosphere, the oceans help regulate global climate, storing excess heat in summer and releasing it in winter. They are a source of life-sustaining rainfall and contribute food, minerals and energy, as well as offering avenues for commerce, a repository for humanity's wastes and a setting for conflict and war.

From the distant perspective of a space voyager, the oceans look grand and immobile. In fact, they are extraordinarily dynamic, scoured by storms and stirred

The storm-tossed waters of the Atlantic display the restless nature of the oceans. While steady winds propel currents that meander across the ocean's surface, storm winds whip the topmost water into waves. Meanwhile, great masses of water rise and sink, propelled by variations in density and temperature, in a complex three-dimensional structure.

by the daily ebb and flow of the tides. Steadier winds, created by Earth's rotation and the warming rays of the Sun, power the surface currents—great corridors in the sea such as the Atlantic's Gulf Stream.

Venturesome explorers have been riding these currents and winds through the ages. The Vikings reached the New World in their beamy, oak and pine *knarrs* 500 years before Christopher Columbus; the Polynesians may have landed on the western coast of South America even earlier. Yet scientists are just starting to appreciate and explain the full diversity of the forces at work inside a global ocean that on average is more than two miles deep. Already they have found complexities far greater than anything imagined by earlier generations of investigators.

Using a host of high-tech instruments—acoustic probes, deep-diving submarines, even satellites—oceanographers have discovered an intricate three-dimensional web of currents below the surface. Propelled by differences in temperature and density, great masses of water rise and fall at a stately pace, traveling through the seas much more languidly than surface currents. Some of them take thousands of years to wend from one end of the planet to the other. Still other currents flow in directions completely opposite to those above or below them. Sometimes these slow, balletic motions erupt in great storms on the ocean floor that may be completely undetected by wayfarers on the calm surface.

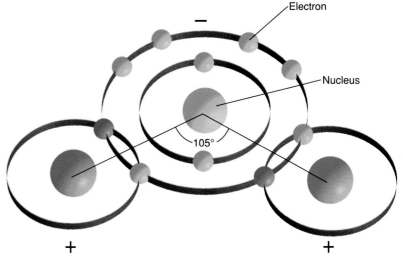

Contemporary oceanographers also have upset the hoary notion of the sea floor as a barren, empty world. In 1841, the British naturalist Edward Forbes had proclaimed that anything below 300 fathoms (1,800 feet) was an azoic or lifeless zone; he happened to have lowered his dredge onto a patch of sea floor in the Eastern Mediterranean that was as sparsely inhabited as any on Earth. But as exploration of the deep sea increased, this bleak picture changed. By the end of the globe-girdling voyage of the British vessel HMS *Challenger* (1872-1876), the first great oceanographic expedition, many living things—eels, sharks, worms, snails and starfish—had been found at hitherto unimaginable depths and pressures. Now we know that life in the seas is at least as varied as on land, embracing the tiniest bacteria as well as the largest whales.

And the surprises are still coming. In 1977, while they were poking around the volcanically active sea floor near the Galápagos Islands in the submersible *Alvin*, scientists discovered whole colonies of animals, ranging from simple, single-celled bacteria to complex mollusks and giant red-tipped tube worms six or seven feet long. Living in eternal darkness, these startlingly novel creatures depended not on photosynthesis—the basic biochemical process of life that taps sunlight to make organic compounds out of carbon dioxide and water—but on the hot, sulfur-rich waters escaping from undersea geysers. They owed their survival not to light but to Earth's own internal heat.

Yet as much as scientists have learned about the seas in recent years, many puzzles still remain to challenge them. They are probing the role the oceans play

A MAVERICK COMPOUND
A water molecule is composed of one oxygen atom (blue) and two hydrogen atoms (purple) separated by an angle of 105 degrees. The nucleus of the oxygen atom has a stronger positive charge than the hydrogen nucleus; therefore, the negatively charged electrons are drawn to the oxygen side, giving the oxygen end of the molecule a negative charge. The hydrogen end has a positive charge. Because of this polarity, the hydrogen end of one water molecule links to the oxygen end of another water molecule, forming an extremely strong bond.

in the "greenhouse effect"—the warming stemming from the atmosphere's worrisome accumulation of heat-trapping industrial gases such as carbon dioxide. It must be determined how much of these gases and the excess heat of the atmosphere the seas can absorb and whether this absorption will moderate the anticipated rise in temperature or enhance global warming trends. Other researchers are trying to harness the seas for energy and food production to meet the needs of a growing population. Perhaps even more importantly, still others are attempting to discover how much of civilization's growing mountains of wastes the seas can accept without suffering irrevocable damage. Such critical issues underscore how much is yet unknown about our lifegiving oceans.

THE NATURE OF WATER

Common as it may be, water possesses many rare qualities. Almost the perfect solvent, it easily soaks up other substances, including the salts found in seawater. In seeming defiance of gravity, it creeps up tiny hollows of trees as tall as giant redwoods. It is the only substance that exists naturally on Earth in solid, liquid and gaseous states—sometimes simultaneously at the same place, as when ice, water and a vaporous mist appear together at a pond or river. For changes of state to occur, however, water must shed or absorb large amounts of energy. This makes it a better storehouse of heat than any other liquid and explains why large masses of water help moderate climate, something that is immediately apparent to anyone who lives in a seaside community during winter.

Equally extraordinary is that water is lighter as a solid than it is as a liquid, which accounts for the fact that ice floats. If it were not for this very special trait, ice would sink to the bottom of the world's rivers, lakes and seas, where it would be shielded from the Sun's thawing radiation, and these bodies of water would become frozen blocks. In summer only the surface layers would melt. On a global scale, this would have devastating consequences: there would then be no ocean surface currents to spread heat from equatorial regions to the poles. The tropics would become unbearably hot and for much of the year, the temperate zones would be assailed by freezing temperatures. Life, as we know it, would be impossible.

Recognizing water's importance, the Greek philosopher Aristotle, in the fourth Century B.C., considered it one of the four "elemental" building blocks of matter, along with earth, fire and air. In the right proportions, he argued, all other materials could be created out of these four, even gold—thereby fanning the dreams of generations of alchemists.

That idea lingered on until 1781 when the Englishman Joseph Priestley performed a paradigmatic experiment—"to entertain a few philosophical friends," he said modestly—that finally illustrated that water itself was a mixture. Igniting ordinary air and what was then called "inflammable air" inside an enclosed vessel, he produced water. Subsequently, Antoine Lavoisier, whose head would soon tumble in the French Revolution, provided its formula: one part oxygen (the major ingredient of air) for every two parts hydrogen (his name for inflammable air).

Water's remarkable—indeed, life-giving—characteristics originate in the very special way these components combine. Rather than linking up with the single oxygen atom by flanking it on either side, the two hydrogen atoms join the oxygen at nearly a right angle. A lopsided configuration, certainly, but one with enormous

THE HEAT ENGINE

Two simple facts help drive the oceans' surface and deep currents. The Earth is 93 million miles distant from the Sun and the Earth spins on its axis.

The Sun's rays strike the world unequally—obliquely at the poles and directly at the Equator. The equatorial region is therefore warmer than the planet's southern and northern extremes. The heat—absorbed by the oceans—is transferred to the overlying air, which creates the wind patterns that drive the surface currents. Those currents are, in turn, twisted into huge gyres by the rotation of the Earth, spinning clockwise north of the Equator and counterclockwise south of it.

At the same time, another Sun-powered circulation of water is at work. A vertical movement of water, called thermohaline circulation, depends on the differences of temperature and density of the water. As cold water at the poles freezes, salt is expelled from the ice; the remaining dense, salty brew sinks from the surface toward the bottom of the ocean. Its place is taken by warm water from the Equator in a gigantic conveyor belt that makes the deep ocean as much a place of unrest as the turbulent domain of the wind-driven currents on the surface.

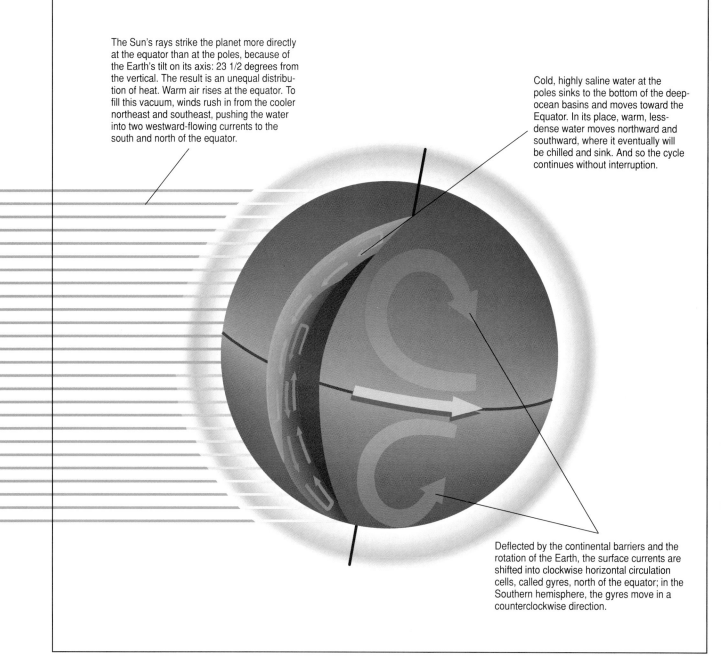

The Sun's rays strike the planet more directly at the equator than at the poles, because of the Earth's tilt on its axis: 23 1/2 degrees from the vertical. The result is an unequal distribution of heat. Warm air rises at the equator. To fill this vacuum, winds rush in from the cooler northeast and southeast, pushing the water into two westward-flowing currents to the south and north of the equator.

Cold, highly saline water at the poles sinks to the bottom of the deep-ocean basins and moves toward the Equator. In its place, warm, less-dense water moves northward and southward, where it eventually will be chilled and sink. And so the cycle continues without interruption.

Deflected by the continental barriers and the rotation of the Earth, the surface currents are shifted into clockwise horizontal circulation cells, called gyres, north of the equator; in the Southern hemisphere, the gyres move in a counterclockwise direction.

chemical consequences. The molecule is polar—people have compared the molecule's appearance to the head of Mickey Mouse—with a negatively charged oxygen "face" and positively charged hydrogen "ears." The "ears"—the hydrogen atoms—arc positively charged; the "face"—the oxygen atom—is negatively charged. The result is that the negative hydrogens act like tiny magnets and attract the positive oxygens of neighboring molecules to form clusters, bound strongly together. Liquid water typically consists of groups of four molecules, ice eight.

Water's "hydrogen bonds" are so powerful that even in its liquid state insects can walk blithely across its surface. And only a prodigious effort can break the bonds, which happens when water boils, or form new ones, as happens when water freezes. A good thing, too: If water consisted of single, unbonded molecules, its freezing and boiling points—0°C (32°F) and 100°C (212°F) at sea level, respectively—would be as much as 200°C (390°F) lower. And the oceans would boil away, leaving behind a sizzling, cloud-covered inferno like Venus.

Water's strong internal structure also accounts for the oceans' immense capacity for storing heat. To raise the temperature of water even slightly requires the addition of enormous quantities of heat; similarly, only a small drop in temperature means the removal of huge amounts of heat. Melting even a small iceberg demands as much energy, in the form of heat, as would be needed to propel a large ocean liner across the Altantic 100 times.

The water molecule has an affinity not only for its own kind, but for other materials as well. This explains why the oceans are salty. Almost as soon as individual elements, including salts, enter the sea—from mid-ocean springs, volcanic eruptions and the runoff of rainwater from the land—they vanish into solution, like a cube of sugar in a cup of hot coffee. In liquids without water's special properties, they would settle out. The salt, in turn, imposes changes of its own. It reduces the freezing point of water slightly, down to -2°C (29°F), and makes it somewhat denser—until it actually freezes, whereupon the water abruptly becomes lighter. As this point, it also expels the salt, leaving it behind to concentrate in the remaining unfrozen water. Since it is denser, this salty brew sinks and slides into deeper layers of the ocean.

Because of water's affinity for other molecules, the oceans also dissolve large quantities of atmospheric oxygen and carbon dioxide, including those from fossil fuels, thereby moderating the greenhouse effect. But the oceans already contain 50 times more carbon dioxide than the atmosphere, and scientists wonder how much more can be soaked up. It is not an idle concern: In some of their "worst case" greenhouse scenarios, average temperatures will climb 9°F by the middle of the next century, thus melting a significant percentage of the polar icecaps and causing a rise in sea level of about a meter (3.2 feet).

The oceans, of course, contain much more than carbon dioxide, oxygen and salt. Just about all the elements found on Earth are dissolved in the sea, including precious metals, if only in trace amounts. After World War I, the German oceanographic vessel *Meteor* looked for gold from the sea to pay off Germany's war debt. What was found was too insignificant to extract commercially, but more recently sea water has come to public attention for another treasure it might yield: enough fresh water to slake the thirst of parched communities around the world. The seaside town of Santa Barbara, California (population 100,000), stunned by years of drought, has decided to harvest the bountiful Pacific right at its front door. Most large desalination plants are expensive, energy-intensive distilleries, which repeatedly vaporize and condense sea water until it becomes pure enough to drink. But Santa Barbara's new $25-million facility, from which it hopes to get a third of its drinking water by 1992, relies on a technology that requires no heat. It is called reverse osmosis, and it works with all the simplicity of an experiment in a high school chemistry laboratory.

If sea water and fresh water are separated by a slightly porous membrane, the molecules of water tend to flow through the barrier into the salty side to equalize the concentration of water molecules. But if the saltwater is pumped past the semipermeable membrane under high pressure, salts, bacteria and unwanted solids are trapped on one side while water molecules pass through the membrane and collect on the other side. It takes two or three gallons of sea water to produce one gallon of fresh water by this method, and the cost is two or three times that of water from natural resources such as lakes and rivers, but it is a price more and more communities may be willing to pay for such liquid "gold" from the sea.

POWERED BY THE SUN

Though the Sun's nuclear fires are raging 93 million miles away, they are the biosphere's ultimate heat engine, driving most planetary processes, including the restless movements of the oceans. As the Sun's rays beat down upon the water, the heat and resulting evaporation help set it in motion. In combination with Earth's rotation, solar heating also stirs the global winds, which in turn create the large-scale motions of oceanic currents.

Solar energy falls upon Earth at a prodigious rate—130 trillion horsepower of energy per second. About 30 percent of the incoming radiation is bounced directly back to space. The remainder is absorbed by the planet, soaked up by the atmosphere or the Earth's surface. After fueling the world's weather machine, including the currents in the atmosphere and the sea, and sustaining the planet's myriad forms of life, the solar radiation is reradiated as infrared. Four percent (of the original 70 percent) returns unimpeded to the void; the rest follows after some back-and-forth interactions with the atmosphere. In this way, Earth balances its energy budget—the amount of energy coming in and going out—repaying the energy it receives. If this were not the case, Earth would heat up, and global temperatures would climb uncomfortably from the current average of 57°F at the surface.

Still, the balance is a delicate one. It could be upset by even a small change in the planet's albedo, the ability of the atmosphere and surface to reflect incoming light. While the oceans reflect no more than 10 to 15 percent of the light that strikes them, snow and ice bounce back as much as 80 percent. Thus, if the polar icecaps expanded, the planet's overall albedo would increase sharply, more rays would be reflected into the void and the average global temperature would drop. An increase in the area covered by the world's deserts would produce a similar effect.

Earth's temperature also is sensitive to changes in so-called greenhouse gases, such as carbon dioxide, water vapor and methane. Like the glass panes of a greenhouse, these atmospheric gases are largely transparent to the Sun's incoming short-wavelength radiation, but relatively opaque to outgoing infrared, or heat, waves, which are longer. If the amount of gases increased—from industrial emissions, for instance—they would trap more heat and raise global surface temperatures. The Sun's heat is felt most powerfully in the equatorial regions, not only because the solar rays strike from directly overhead, and hence are not deflected or spread over a larger area, but also because they pass through less atmosphere. Even so, the amount of sunlight falling on any portion of the planet at any time of the year varies seasonally because of the 23 1/2° tilt of the Earth's axis of rotation from the vertical. Thus, as the planet makes its annual voyage around the Sun, for part of the year the Northern Hemisphere gets more sunlight and for part the Southern Hemisphere is the chief beneficiary of its warming rays.

Though solar heating causes equatorial air to rise, creating atmospheric circulation and prevailing winds, it also has a significant effect on equatorial waters. The Sun's rays evaporate fresh water from the surface, making the tropical air steamy, and leaving behind a much saltier brew. Ordinarily, heavy, salt-rich water would sink, but in this case it is also expanded by the heat of the scorching Sun, creating a flow away from the Equator. The heated water, however, is quickly intercepted by the prevailing winds and deflected into two westward-flowing currents immediately north and south of the Equator.

At the poles, the Sun's much weaker rays have the opposite effect. In the intense cold, the surface water, already more salty after the ice has formed, becomes so dense that it sinks deep into the ocean. There it displaces the existing bottom water, which is forced slowly upward in a general flow toward the Equator and then migrates back to the sinking regions, altered only by the shape of the sea floor and Earth's rotation. Such movements are significantly different than the usual surface currents. Impelled by differences in water temperature and salinity, rather than by wind, these movements are termed thermohaline circulation. The system works in a conveyor belt-like motion that moves millions of gallons of water per second from the Equator toward the poles and back again in a global pageant that takes centuries to make one circuit.

The two principal thermohaline cells are the Antarctic Bottom Water (AABW) and the North Atlantic Deep Water (NADW). Central to the former is the Weddell Sea, a large embayment along the coast of Antarctica directly south of the Atlantic Ocean, where the harsh weather and quirky surface flows create the densest, saltiest ocean water in the world. As pack ice forms, most of the salt is expelled from the ice's crystalline structure, leaking as a cold brine into the sea water just underneath. Frigid winds from Antarctica's interior chill the water further and make it even more dense. Sliding down the continental slope, the unusually cold, salty water mixes with the oceans' deep circulation, which carries it toward the Equator and beyond. Antarctic Bottom Water carpets the greatest depths of much of the world's oceans. It has been detected as far north as the edges of the Grand Banks near Newfoundland in the North Atlantic, and in the Pacific up to the Aleutian Islands off the coast of Alaska.

Overlapping the northward flow of the Antarctic Bottom Water, the North Atlantic "conveyor" flows southward and spreads into the Indian and Pacific Oceans. The water mass is the result of northward-flowing warm water in the Atlantic Ocean that is made salty and dense because of evaporation and chilling. The main contributor to the flow comes from the Greenland and Norwegian Seas. As relatively warm water flows with the surface Norwegian Current into the two seas it sinks into the deep basin north of a submarine ridge that runs from Greenland to Scotland. From there it slips through passages across the ridge and pushes into the deep ocean to the south. Local perturbations also affect deepwater circulation in the North Atlantic, most notably in the eastern part of the ocean, where an enormous tongue of extremely saline water from the Mediterranean Sea makes a major intrusion.

The cold deep-sea movements are extremely languid. It may take 2,000 years for a molecule of water that sank off Antarctica to return there and eventually be returned to the surface by a continual upward diffusion of deep water. But that does not make thermohaline circulation any less important. By replacing warm water moving away from the Equator with cold water from the polar seas, it plays a key role in transferring heat across the face of the planet, keeping the polar regions from slipping into a cycle of deepening chills or the tropics from getting warmer and warmer. The influence that thermohaline circulation has in global climate adds an extra dimension to the threat of global warming. Some scientists hypothesize that if the world's temperatures rise several degrees, the polar ice sheets will melt and dilute the salty brew in the polar regions. That, in turn, will slow down or even stop the conveyor belt in the deep ocean with a resulting disastrous impact on the world's weather *(page 134)*.

TRACKING THE CURRENTS
Probably the first person to notice the cold, torpid flow of deep sea water was a British sea captain, Harry Ellis, of the slaveship *Earl of Halifax*. In 1751, when hoisting a bucket of water from the depths off West Africa, he found its contents surprisingly chilly, even though the surface temperature of the sea was warm under the tropical Sun. Told of this briny cooler—in which Ellis chilled his wine—scientists concluded that the deep cold water in these equatorial latitudes could have only a single explanation. It must have originated in the polar regions.

Shrewd as these speculations were, the full extent of the complexity of oceans' deep sea circulation was not fully appreciated for many years, until oceanographers realized that nature provided ideal detectives to follow the intricate loops and whorls of oceanic flows, even those far below the surface. The substances were radioactive isotopes, variants of an element that differ slightly in atomic weight from their more common form. Used as tracers, they told scientists where a sample of water originated and how long since it had last seen the light of day.

One of the most useful isotopes for studying ocean currents is tritium, a very rare variety of hydrogen that was produced in the atmosphere from the atomic bomb tests of the 1950s and 1960s. Since the time and amounts of scattering over the ocean are approximately known, scientists can readily determine how far and at what speed any samples of tritium collected in the sea have traveled. But even if the date of the tritium's oceanic baptismal were unknown, the age of any sample can easily be ascertained from its known rate of decay, or "half-life"—the time it takes half of the original amount of an isotope to disintegrate into a simpler "daughter" element. The scientist merely measures the relative quantities of the isotope and daughter element, which in the case of tritium is helium-3. If a given sample of water happens to contain one part helium for every part tritium, the sample must be 12 years old, because tritium's half-life is 12 years. If the ratio

A SLICE OF WATER

As shown in this idealized illustration, ocean water is in constant motion, not just on its surface, but right to the sea floor. Because of variations in temperature and density, ocean water is stratified in distinct horizontal layers that move independently of each other. Water at the surface is exposed to the Sun and wind and is therefore the warmest and fastest-moving layer of ocean water. Beneath that, water becomes increasingly cooler and slower moving with depth. As water cools or as its salt content increases, it becomes more dense and sinks below the lighter surface layers and settles in ever-thickening layers. Only at the top layer and at continental margins are these watery sheets disrupted by vertical-moving water.

Oceanographers have recently discovered other movements that are testament to the ocean's restlessness. Although the ocean surface is constantly animated by waves, it is not their sole domain. Immense waves have been detected traveling along undersea layers. They are many times higher than the highest surface waves, yet move more slowly. Also, gigantic rotating funnels of water known as rings—sometimes as large as 200 miles across—form from meandering currents and roll through the sea. The rings imprison and transport cores of water that may be cooler or warmer than the surrounding water.

Surface Current
Driven by winds that are, in turn, the product of the Sun's heat, surface currents are capable of transporting million of gallons of water every second.

Cold Core Ring
Formed when a strong surface current such as the Gulf Stream meanders enough to encircle a body of water from the northern side of the current until it pinches off entirely in a perfect ring or eddy. The same can happen on the south side so that the meander entraps a warm core of water in its ring.

Deep Sound Channel
A temperate layer of water, approximately 4,000 feet deep, with a density that permits optimum travel conditions for sound. During a 1960 experiment, depth charges sounded in a channel off the coast of Australia were detected by hydrophones off the coast of Bermuda three-and-a-half hours later —12,000 miles away.

Internal Wave
Can form at the boundaries of subsurface layers and attain heights as high as 300 feet, three times the height of the highest surface waves. Although not well understood, internal waves are thought to be caused by factors such as tidal currents, underwater avalanches and energy created underwater by moving vessels.

Deep Ocean Current
A cold, salty—and therefore dense—layer of ocean water. It moves so slowly from the poles that it takes hundreds of years to traverse the ocean and resurface near the Equator and along continental margins it encounters along the way.

Deep Scattering Layer
A phenomenon produced by large masses of shrimplike crustaceans that scatter and reflect sonar signals at a depth near 3,000 feet, well above the average ocean floor depth. This layer migrates more than 1,000 feet upward at night to feed on smaller planktonic organisms, and then retreats during the day to escape the jaws of larger prey.

increases to two parts helium for every part tritium, this means two-thirds of the original tritium has decayed, and the sample is half again as old, or 18 years.

However, the age of the water in some deep sea currents greatly exceeds the half-life of tritium, so isotopes with longer half-lives must be used. One common tracer is carbon-14, a radioactive isotope of ordinary stable carbon with a half-life of 5,560 years. It is particularly valuable for identifying organic materials dissolved in sea water, since they are rich in carbon and contain its isotopes.

More recently, ocean scientists have been turning to a completely different sort of tracer: Freon, or CFC (chlorofluorocarbon), the highly stable manmade compound used as a refrigerant and aerosol propellant (and a prime suspect in the destruction of Earth's protective ozone shield). Though its manufacture is now being curtailed under international agreement, it remains highly useful to oceanographers because it enters the seas from the atmosphere at a known rate (proportional to the production rate in factories) and spreads through the oceans unaltered by biological processes or radioactive decay.

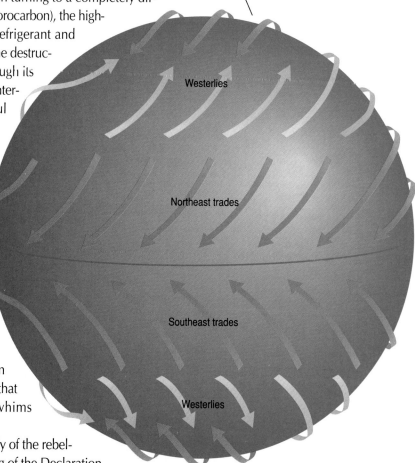

BORNE BY THE WIND

Although spacecraft now can circle Earth in 90 minutes, zipping along at 17,000 miles per hour, it was not so long ago that even the fastest ships took a month or even more to cross the Atlantic Ocean. Indeed, until the advent of the steam engine, not only ships, but also the empires that sailed those ships were subject to the whims of winds and currents.

England's George III did not learn officially of the rebellion of his American Colonies and the signing of the Declaration of Independence on July 4, 1776 until more than a month later because it took that long to get a copy to him. Andrew Jackson, who would be catapulted to the White House by his overwhelming victory in the Battle of New Orleans on January 8, 1815, actually fought it needlessly. A peace treaty with Britain had been signed in Ghent on Christmas Eve 1814, but word had not reached him.

In the great age of sail, no one knew better than the era's master mariners how unpredictable nature could be. But by seeking out regular patterns in winds, weather and ocean currents, they could turn the odds a little more in their favor. It paid off, for instance, to carry cargo from Europe to the New World via a southerly route, catching the prevailing northeasterly winds—the tradewinds or "trades" as they came to be called—which would blow sailing ships all the way to the West Indies. But to get back, mariners had to try a different tact. Setting a more northerly course, they rode a powerful current that would become known as the Gulf Stream until they reached a latitude where they encountered favorable winds so steady they

THE WORLD'S WINDS AND THE CURVING CORIOLIS EFFECT

This simplified drawing (left) shows the global circulation of the winds that drive the ocean's surface currents. The winds in the Northern Hemisphere bend to the right; the reverse happens in the Southern Hemisphere. Both are the result of the Coriolis effect, a force that can be observed in miniature (below) by placing a circular piece of cardboard on a phonograph turntable and spinning it in a counterclockwise direction, which is the direction of the Earth's spin in the Northern Hemisphere. A line drawn with a pencil along the straight edge of a stationary ruler from the center to the circumference describes an arc to the right. The effect stems from the fact that the center of the turntable —like the poles—is stationary while the outside edge—or the equator—is spinning. (On Earth, the equator spins at approximately 1,000 miles per hour.) As the line is drawn, the cardboard disc—moving ever faster towards its circumference—spins out from underneath the pencil.

were called "the westerlies." Flouting these patterns could spell trouble. Any sailor worth his salt knew that a westward crossing of the North Atlantic against the boisterous westerlies could be exceedingly difficult and dangerous. Unable to steer any closer than 66° of the wind, ships of the day had to beat—zigzag—continually to make any forward progress, multiplying the miles and the probability of navigational error, as the *Mayflower* and her Pilgrim passengers learned when they landed in Massachusetts on November 11, 1620, rather than in Virginia, for which they had set out.

In the zones where prevailing winds meet, mariners encountered conditions of a different sort: winds so fickle and light that the sails barely caught a zephyr. One such belt lay between the trades and the westerlies, in both the Northern and Southern Hemispheres. Seamen called them the "horse latitudes" from the long calms that not only exhausted supplies, but often also were fatal to livestock. Sailing ships might find themselves similarly stalled in a region just north of the Equator dubbed the doldrums, another belt of lackluster winds. By contrast, between 40° and 50°, especially in the Southern Hemisphere, the westerlies were so strong mariners tagged these areas the "roaring forties."

As skilled as sailors became in making use of the prevailing winds, no one could really begin to explain them until well into the 19th Century. By then the new industrial age had brought the first crude efforts to explore natural processes. Drawing from their experiments with heated gases, scientists realized that the atmosphere behaves somewhat like boiling water in a teakettle. Under a hot equatorial Sun, atmospheric gases expand and rise like those in a kettle over a flame and move sideways toward the poles. Meanwhile the cooler, denser air in the subtropical and polar regions sinks and flows toward the Equator to replace the warm rising air. Such heat-propelled movements are called convection currents.

Still, while these ideas gave a rough picture of atmospheric circulation, there was plenty of debate about the details. By the late 19th Century, the oceans occupied a place in the popular imagination similar to that of space today: They represented a mysterious and marvelous world and their far reaches brimmed with the unexpected, such as the strange life forms that had been hauled up during the *Challenger* expedition. Even so basic a question as the cause of currents, much less the winds, divided scholars. Some argued that the seas were stirred into motion by differences in temperature and density. Others believed that the currents were propelled by the prevailing winds.

In fact, both theories were correct. As the discovery of descending salt-weighted masses of cold water in regions such as the Weddell Sea demonstrated, oceanic currents in the deep sea are driven by differences in temperature and density. By contrast, surface currents are due largely to the winds. Yet underlying both types

THE MAKING AND BREAKING OF A WAVE

Waves are energy—released when the wave reaches shore. In a single day, waves crashing onto the world's beaches produce an amount of energy equivalent to a 50-megaton hydrogen bomb.

Ocean waves can transport energy for thousands of miles, although the water itself does not move. The wave form moves forward, not the water molecules. The concept can be observed by watching a buoy floating on the ocean surface, bobbing up and down as a wave passes.

Most waves result from wind ruffling an open stretch of water. The area of open water the wind can blow over—the fetch—and the strength of the wind are directly proportional to wave height. A 40-mile per hour wind blowing over a 12-mile stretch of water can produce waves eight feet high; over 60 miles of water, the same

wind will produce waves 14 feet high. Although waves rarely exceed 40 feet, a storm in the Pacific Ocean in 1933 generated waves that were 112 feet high.

Scientists have tried unsuccessfully to harness waves' tremendous energy. One device called the Salter's Duck consists of a hollow float of reinforced concrete 100 feet long and 60 feet wide. Inside the shaft, pumps activated by the rocking motion of the waves power an electric generator. Prototypes have been tested but, like other wave-power facilities, the device has not been able to offer electricity at prices competitive with conventional power stations.

Thundering waves in the Pacific Ocean release pent-up energy after traveling for hundreds of uninterrupted miles. As the waves collapse, small air bubbles are formed, permitting oxygen and other gases to mix into the sea.

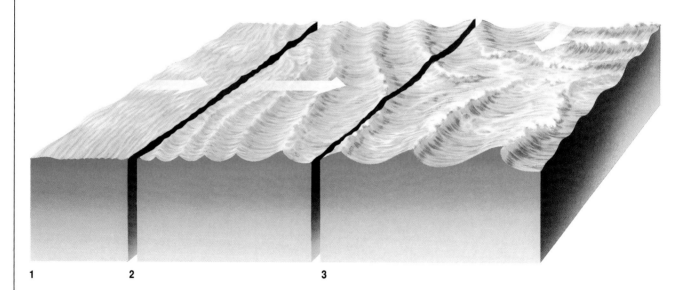

1   **2**   **3**

BIRTH OF A WAVE

1. Wind blowing across open water breaks surface tension, resulting in the formation of ripples. Next, wind catches the ripple's leading edge and pushes against it, reinforcing the wave's form.

2. Wind speeds up over the top of a wave, and slows down in the hollow between two waves, creating areas of uneven air pressure. Wave height is increased as water is pushed downward by high pressure in the trough and drawn upward at the crest by low pressure.

3. As the waves grow, their crests steepen as they grow taller faster than they grow longer. If the crest attains a critical angle —120 degrees—the steepness of the wave causes it to become unstable and the wave breaks, producing whitecaps.

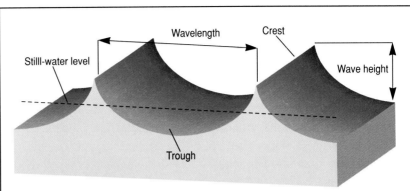

Wavelength

Crest

Stilll-water level

Wave height

Trough

THE ANATOMY OF A WAVE

All waves—in air or in water—can be described as alternating crests and troughs. The height from a crest, or high part of the wave, to the trough, low part of the wave, is the wave height. The distance between two consecutive crests—which can range from a few feet to a mile—is called the wavelength. Many wave characteristics can be explained by arithmetical relationships. A whitecap, for example, forms when the wave height is one-seventh of a wavelength, producing a wave with a crest that has an angle of 120 degrees. And a wave breaks when the depth of the water is 1⅓ times the height of the wave.

A Spilling Breaker
Once the wave approaches shore it "feels" ground. Friction causes the lower portion of the wave to slow down, while the upper portion continues to move at the original speed. Curling over, the top of the wave soon breaks off from the bottom, producing a breaker. If the wave rolls onto a gently sloping bottom, it expends its energy slowly, producing what is known as a spilling breaker.

A Plunging Breaker
On a steeper shore, incoming waves soon encounter water too shallow to sustain them. The wave crests arch forward and envelop air pockets as they collapse before retreating as backwash.

A Surging Breaker
On a very steep shore, waves heave up in the shallow water and collapse into themselves as the base of the wave outruns the crest, producing a foamy sheet of swash that undermines the wave form.

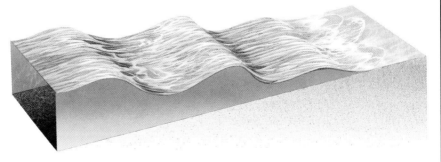

of currents is an even more basic phenomenon: the unequal heating of Earth by the Sun. If the Sun shone as strongly at the poles as it does at the Equator, then the waters of the Weddell Sea would not sink from cooling, nor would there exist the winds to power immense currents such as the Gulf Stream. The water of the world's oceans would remain in place.

In the simplest of worlds—on an Earth that did not rotate—atmospheric circulation would consist of two giant convection cells. Two great streams of air would travel in opposing directions from the Equator to the poles and back again. On such a motionless planet, surface winds would blow from the north in the Northern Hemisphere and from the south in the Southern Hemisphere. But Earth does rotate. And as the French mathematician Gaspard Gustave de Coriolis (1792-1843) was to point out, Earth's rotation vastly complicates winds and currents.

Humans are not aware of these complications in their daily lives. When someone tosses a ball at a target, for instance, it travels in a more-or-less straight line except for the dip caused by the tug of gravity. But if the ball is thrown from a moving platform—rotating counterclockwise as Earth does (as viewed from the North Pole)—it appears to veer to the right of the target, which is also on the moving platform. (In the Southern Hemisphere, where Earth's rotation would be ascertained from the South Pole, it would be considered to be spinning clockwise and the ball's motion would be to the left.) The ball, of course, is traveling in the same straight line as before; it is the target that has moved during the ball's flight.

Something similar happens to ocean currents and winds. As they travel away from the Equator in the Northern Hemisphere, they are deflected to the right because of Earth's counterclockwise rotation. In the Southern Hemisphere, the displacement is toward the left because Earth's clockwise rotation there. If these deflections could be traced on the rotating Earth's surface, they would be visible as large circular motions.

This effect, named after Coriolis, influences not only the winds blowing over the waters of the oceans, but also the movement of the water underneath the surface—a fact that was discovered by happenstance by Fridtjof Nansen, a late 19th-Century Norwegian Arctic explorer, who practiced science with meticulous care. To find out whether there was land or a sea at the North Pole—still a great scientific issue in his time—he built an extraordinary ship that could carry him safely into the ice-crusted Arctic Sea, if in fact there was one. To survive encounters with the ice, its hull was built of planks four feet thick and encased in a wood called greenheart, which was so dense it did not float. Nansen hoped that his ship would be able to "slip like an eel out of the embrace of the ice."

On July 27, 1893, his sturdy ship, christened *Fram* (Norwegian for "forward"), headed for the Arctic. Within three months, the 128-foot schooner and its 13-member crew were locked completely in the polar ice. The *Fram* did not break free until the summer of 1896. But in those three years, the ship continued to move. Careful sextant sightings showed that it had drifted 1,028 miles, mostly to the southwest, averaging about a mile a day. These results confirmed Nansen's belief that there was an ocean at the top of the world, and that its covering of ice moved with this sea's currents. But the voyage also posed a puzzle. *Fram* had not drifted with prevailing winds, but rather some 20° to 40° to the right of them, a deviation that Nansen ascribed to the Coriolis effect.

Again his scientific instincts were accurate. Studying the data from *Fram's* voyage, the Swedish physicist and oceanographer Vagn Walfrid Ekman evolved a mathematical model to account for the perplexing movements. In 1905 he showed that as a wind blows steadily over the ocean, the Coriolis effect diverts the motion of the topmost "layer" of water at an angle of about 45° to the right of the wind's direction in the Northern Hemisphere (and to the left in the Southern Hemisphere). Lower layers are set in motion as well, though with progressively less and less force at increasing depth because of the slippage between water molecules. Thus the water's velocity not only slows down, but also its angle to the wind becomes larger in successive layers, giving them the appearance of steps on a spiral staircase, each one a little bit to the right of the previous. Finally, at about 300 feet, the water has done a complete reversal, moving in a direction opposite to that at the surface. Such a twisting water column under a windblown sea is named after its discoverer and is called an Ekman spiral.

In practice, oceanographers never find water behaving exactly as predicted by Ekman's theoretical model; sea conditions are much too chaotic. But Ekman flows, giving the various layers of water an overall spin at right angles to the wind, are real enough and their effects can be observed not only by ships trapped in the Arctic, but elsewhere as well. One notable example occurs along the coast of California, where prevailing winds, plus an Ekman spiral, sweep warm surface water offshore; and deep, colder water rises in its place, bringing with it a host of nutrients that create fertile fishing grounds (and not incidentally California's infamous coastal fogs when the chilly water meets warm, moist summer winds). Similar nutrient-rich, fog-creating upwellings occur off the coast of Peru.

The discovery of the Ekman spiral also settled another argument about the oceans. In the middle of the 19th Century, an American schoolteacher and physicist, William Ferrel, had predicted that one effect of Earth's rotation on warm equatorial waters would be to pile it up in midocean, creating a little hill about five feet above sea level at the Equator. Under the weight of this hill, deep water would be pushed away from the Equator.

Ferrel did not have it quite right; the hills do not form at the Equator. But, as Ekman showed, under the spiraling effect of Earth's rotation, the prevailing winds do build a mound of water as much as six feet high near the center of each ocean basin north and south of the Equator. These act as the hubs of the great gyres of current encircling the basins.

Deflected to the right by the winds, the upper layers of water in each basin tend to move northward of the trade winds and southward of the westerlies. Thus, water levels build up in the calmer latitudes between them. Obeying the immutable law of gravity, the elevated water tends to flow downhill, but as it does, the Coriolis effect bends it as well (to the right in the Northern Hemisphere and the reverse in the Southern), producing a large circular flow around the central mound.

In still another byproduct of Earth's rotation, the hub is displaced slightly to the left, an idea first postulated in 1947 by Henry Stommel, a young oceanographer at Massachusetts' Woods Hole Oceanographic Institution, and later confirmed by actual measurements. The consequences of this offset are major: The water flowing toward the pole on the western side of the gyre is more tightly pressed against the adjacent continent than the opposing currents flowing toward the Equator on the much broader and deeper eastern side of the gyre, and thus must move much faster. The result can be seen in such powerful currents as the Gulf Stream, in the western North Atlantic, and the Kuroshio (Black Current), in the North Pacific off Japan, which speed at velocities of five knots or more along the western side of their respective ocean basins.

Gyres are found in each of the world's oceans. Driven by the prevailing winds they rotate clockwise in the Northern Hemisphere and counterclockwise in the Southern hemisphere. The Kuroshio, for example, is part of the North Pacific Gyre. And like the Gulf Stream, it is really only the fast-flowing western edge—or western boundary current, in the precise language of oceanography—of its parent gyre. If these waters were not blocked by the continents, each belt of winds would whip a corresponding flow of current all the way around the planet. Only in the chilly waters around Antarctica, with no terrestrial obstacle in their path, does a current completely circle the globe, helping to isolate the icy continent from warming waters and making it the coldest place on Earth.

EYES IN THE SKY

Measuring variations in elevation of a few feet over hundreds of miles on land is a challenging task; on the shifting face of the ocean it is an even more difficult enterprise—a fact that underscores how oceanography has been revolutionized in recent years. For decades the only way to ferret out the secrets of the oceans was to go to sea. From the rolling decks of small research vessels, oceanographers hauled up water from selected depths—in special bottles named after Nansen, the intrepid Norwegian who devised them—took temperature readings, measured salinity and launched buoys. It was slow, arduous and, when the seas rose up in 30-foot-high waves, dangerous work. No less an oceanographer than Maurice Ewing, founder of the Lamont-Doherty Geophysical Observatory, was nearly lost at sea when a giant wave crashed over the research vessel *Vema* during a winter gale in the 1950s and swept him and three colleagues overboard. One was lost.

With the Space Age came a safer and far more sophisticated—though far more costly—method of studying the oceans. Only a few years after the Soviet Union launched the first Earth satellite in 1957, unmanned spacecraft were providing astonishing pictures of cloud formations, mountain ranges and rain forests, even ocean currents from a perspective never before available to earthbound observers.

For oceanographers, no satellite opened more remarkable vistas than a pioneering spacecraft called *Seasat*, the first to be dedicated exclusively to the oceans. Launched in 1978 into a near-polar orbit, at almost right angles to the plane of the Equator, it looped from the Arctic to Antarctica and back again every 100 minutes at an altitude of more than 500 miles. As Earth rotated underneath it, its instruments completed a survey of the entire planet every 17 days.

One of those instruments was a radar altimeter. By reflecting a narrow beam of microwaves off the surface of the sea, and precisely timing their roundtrip between the wave tops and the satellite, the instrument could measure the height of particular parts of the ocean down to an accuracy of two or three inches. Never before had anyone been able to make such precise measurements of the sea.

Seasat operated for only 104 days before it was blinded by a massive onboard electrical failure. But in that time it made 1,000 orbits of Earth and some eight

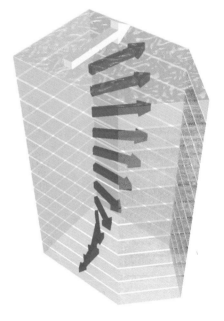

THE EKMAN SPIRAL
As wind drives surface currents (top arrow), the underlying water is set in motion by friction and deflected by the Coriolis effect. With increasing depth each layer is deflected more and moves more slowly, until at about 300 feet a weak current is moving in a direction opposite to the wind (bottom arrow). The overall result of this so-called Ekman spiral is to move water at right angles to the wind.

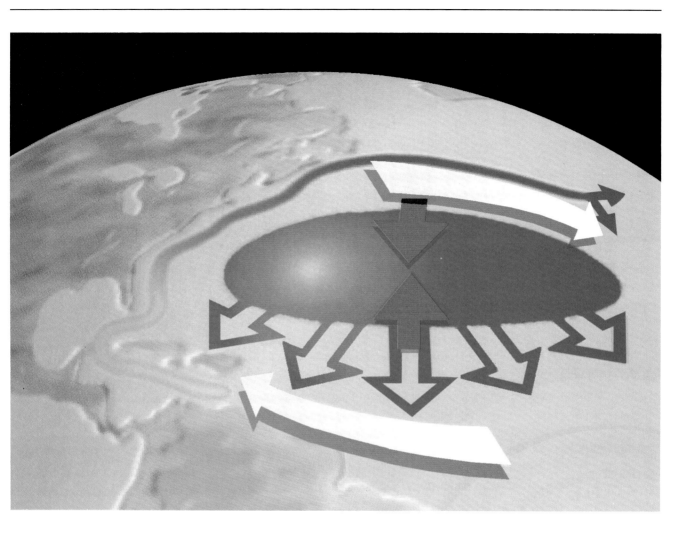

PILING UP THE WATER

In the North Atlantic the Ekman spiral pushes water to the right in conjunction with prevailing winds. These flows push the ocean surface into a mound several feet high and hundreds of miles across, its center—shown as a light spot—shifted to the left of the middle of the gyre by the rotation of the Earth. The extra weight of the hump pushes downward and squeezes it outward, reducing its speed of rotation. As a consequence, the water moves toward the Equator, where the Earth's rotation matches its new speed. The displaced water is replaced by a return flow that runs along the western shore of the ocean—the Gulf Stream.

billion separate measurements of the sea surface. Among other things, these showed that there was an average rise of 4.7 feet from the outer to the inner edge of the Gulf Stream, confirming the presence of a mound in the middle of the ocean. It found other deviations from sea level as well. Over large seamounts—ancient undersea volcanoes whose tops have often been eroded away by waves—the water was piled up as much as 30 feet above the surrounding sea; the water was being pulled toward the submerged mountains by their gravity. Over deep-sea trenches—the product of massive downward movements of sections of the sea floor—the satellite discovered hollows instead of hills, some of them 30 feet deep. Hidden by waves, tides and currents, not to mention a vessel's own wake, these ups and downs in the open sea cannot be observed from a ship. But from its synoptic viewpoint high above Earth, a satellite with the appropriate sensors and equipment has no trouble spotting these and other elusive aspects of the sea.

Inspired by the stunning if abbreviated performance of *Seasat*, the National Aeronautics and Space Administration (NASA) joined with the French Space Agency to develop a double-barreled successor called TOPEX/POSEIDON—the first name an acronym for NASA's Topography of Ocean Experiment; the second a Gallic bow to the ancient Greek god of the sea. Scheduled for launch in 1992, the satellite boasts a powerful radar altimeter capable of measuring sea height with a margin of error of less than an inch. By observing the wind's effect on the sea

A CELESTIAL TUG OF WAR

The two high tides that occur every day stem not from winds or the regular forces that produce waves; rather they are the result of the difference between the pull of the Moon's gravity and the Earth's centrifugal force. The connection between the Moon and the tides has long been recognized. Writing in 330 B.C., the Greek philosopher Aristotle observed, "It is even said that many ebbings and rising of the sea always come round with the moon and on certain fixed days."

Every material thing in the universe is attracted by gravity to everything else. The nearer the objects are to each other and the greater the masses, the more powerful the attraction between them. As the moon makes its 24-hour-and-50-minute orbit around the Earth it exerts a gravitational pull, tugging at its parent planet. The deformation of the solid Earth is too small to be noticed except by the most sensitive of instruments, but the pull on the oceans raises the water into a bulge that travels with the Moon's rotation around the world.

On the side of the Earth facing away from the Moon, another bulge in the ocean is formed by the Earth's centrifugal force, which overwhelms the force of gravity. Centrifugal force is the result of the Earth's rotation, which tends to pull an object away from a spinning center. The ocean is, in a sense, "pulled" outward away from the Earth much as the water in a bucket being swung at the end of a rope is forced outward and stays in its container.

The Sun also plays its part in the formation of tides—albeit a minor one. Although its mass is far greater than the Moon's, the Sun is almost 400 times farther from the Earth. The solar machine therefore merely augments or diminishes the lunar tides, depending on the alignment of the Earth and the Moon.

Nowhere in the world is the difference between high tide and low tide more pronounced than in Canada's Bay of Fundy. An inlet of the Atlantic Ocean jutting between the provinces of Nova Scotia and New Brunswick, the bay has a funnel shape that accentuates the tidal amplitude—as much as 56 feet a day. Twelve hours after this photograph was taken, when the tide rolled in, all the boats were afloat.

THE TUG ON THE TIDES

With the Moon at right angles to the Sun during quarter moon (1) and (3), the tides are partly offset by the Sun's pull and variation between high and low tides is least. Both are called neap tides. The highest and lowest tides occur when the Moon, Earth and Sun are in alignment. The resulting spring tides occur twice a month—at full moon (2) and new moon (4).

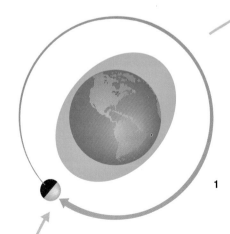

1

HARNESSING THE MOON'S POWER

A tidal-power station takes advantage of the fact that water levels rise and fall with the tides. When the tide rises, the flood of water is channeled into a reservoir (top right). When the tide ebbs, the water is released from the reservoir, driving the blades of a turbine (below).

The idea of generating power from tides is not new. A tidal mill at Dover, England, was mentioned in the Domesday Book, published in 1086. The first power station using tides to generate hydroelectric power was completed across the mouth of the Rance estuary in northern France in 1966. Twice a day, a tidal flow nearly equivalent to that of the Mississippi River pours through 24 turbines situated inside the 2,460-foot-long dam. The submarine-shaped turbines feature reversible blades, generating power during both the tide's ebb and flow. The Rance station produces 240 megawatts, enough to supply Brittany and also to contribute to the demands of Paris.

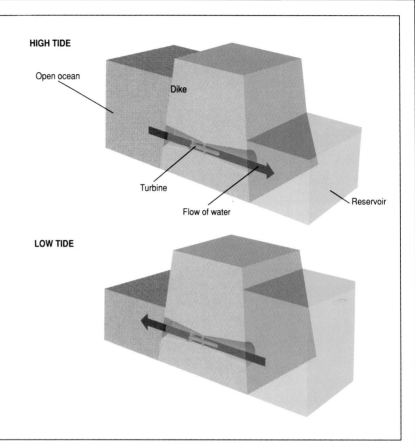

HIGH TIDE

Open ocean

Dike

Turbine

Flow of water

Reservoir

LOW TIDE

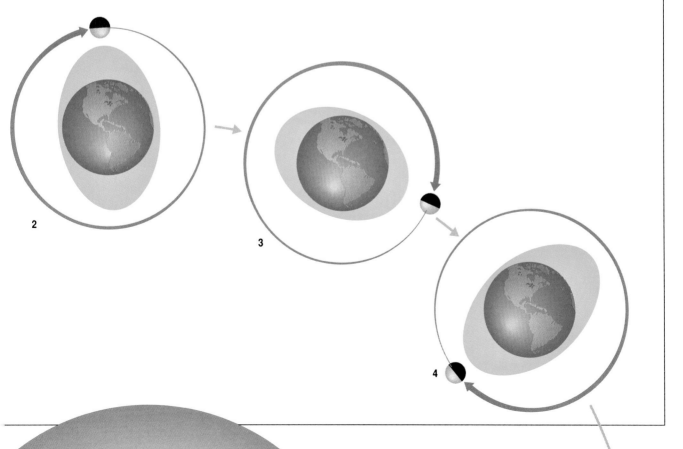

2

3

4

surface, it will also be able to determine wind speed, though not direction. During its anticipated three to five years of operation, TOPEX/POSEIDON should yield maps more accurate than any previously available of oceanic winds and currents, including large-scale stormlike eddies.

Since the start of remote sensing from orbit in the 1960s, satellites have been measuring not only the sea's height, but also its temperature, roughness, currents and ice covering, either through their own electronic eyes or by collecting radioed information from automated buoys. The spacecraft have also turned out to be gifted photographers. Thanks to the image processing capability of computers, individual data points from satellite sensors can be assembled into panoramic color views that show entire ocean basins, including the hostile, storm-tossed areas of Antarctica, where research ships can operate only with greatest effort.

Instead of traveling in polar orbits, many satellites are parked much farther out in space in what are called geostationary orbits. At a distance of 23,300 miles above the Equator, the satellites match the Earth's own speed of rotation and thus seem to hover like helicopters over the same spot on the ground below. As reconnaissance tools, they are able to watch virtually an entire hemisphere, except for the polar regions, and they are able to monitor changes, such as atmospheric or oceanic movements continuously.

Some satellites travel in orbits that are only slightly tilted to the plane formed by the Equator, allowing them to concentrate on tropical regions. The Soviet Union's *Molniya* (Lightning) satellites are launched into highly elongated orbits that take them far out into space, then bring them very close in. The trajectories are calculated to allow the satellites to spend more time over the northern latitudes, in which the bulk of the Soviet Union lies, rather than over outlying equatorial or southern regions. Still other satellites, in near-polar orbits, are also Sun-synchronous: They always travel at the same angle to the Sun and thus always observe an area under the same lighting conditions, regardless of the season.

All sorts of sensors are carried aboard satellites to do oceanographic surveying from space. Some are active, like the radar beacon aboard *Seasat*. Others work passively, collecting various frequencies of light, especially infrared, a measure of heat—and often a clue to biological activity. When NASA launched its Nimbus-7 weather satellite in 1978, it carried a novel sensor called the Coastal Zone Color Scanner (CZCS). The scanner's job was to observe the changing colors of the oceans, especially the murky green-brown tint of chlorophyll, the photosensitive pigment that signals the presence of phytoplankton. These microscopic organisms—sometimes called the grasses of the sea—fulfill the same role as green plants on land. Converting carbon dioxide and water into organic materials, they are the lowest link in the marine food chain.

Over a lifetime of eight years—seven more than anticipated—CZCS performed extraordinarily well, revealing the oceans to be not only far more dynamic, but also more important to the global carbon cycle than anyone had suspected. One surprising discovery was the extent of the phytoplankton "bloom" at high latitudes each spring, caused by the lengthening day.

Earth satellites are also being used to observe individual marine animals, notably whales. "Tagged" with tiny, battery-powered radio transmitters, each of which gives off a distinctive signal, the animals can be followed for months at a time over

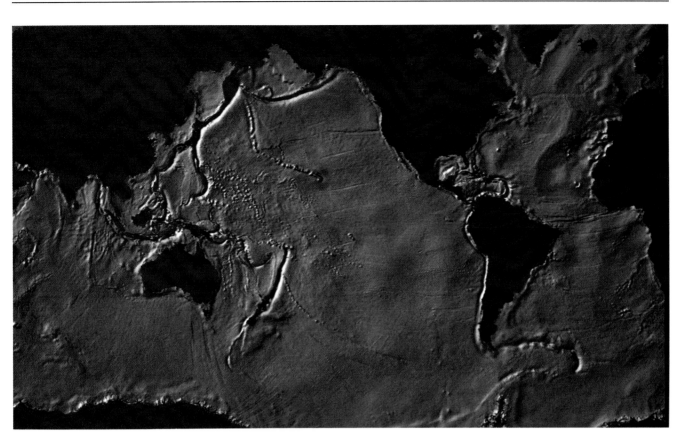

This computer image of the surface of the world's oceans was produced from altimeter data collected by Seasat *during its three-month working life in 1978. The bulges and troughs in the water reflect features on the ocean floor. A submarine concentration of mass, such as the Mid Ocean Ridge, creates a slight increase in gravity that pulls extra water toward it. Undersea trenches, on the other hand, exert a weaker gravitational attraction and produce troughs on the ocean's surface, such as those visible in the western Pacific Ocean—the deepest submarine trenches on the planet. The differences in elevation between the two can be as great as 60 feet.*

thousands of miles of ocean. The satellite picks up the signals, then relays them to a ground station, which identifies the specific whale from its signature beep and locates its position in the sea. These experiments are yielding unique "real-time" information on cetacean migration, diving, sleeping and feeding patterns, none of which could be easily observed from a ship's deck.

THE GULF STREAM

Some years before the American Revolution, while he was in London as agent for the American Colonies, Benjamin Franklin received a puzzling complaint about the transatlantic mail service. British mail packets, he was told, were taking two weeks longer to make the crossing from Falmouth, England, to New York than it took Rhode Island merchantmen to sail from London to Providence. Franklin was puzzled, as he expressed it, "that there should be such a difference between the two destinations, which were scarcely a day's sail apart."

Franklin put the matter to his cousin, a visiting Nantucket whaling captain named Timothy Folger, who was not at all surprised by the delay. He and his fellow whaling captains had often chased whales along the edge of a powerful current, he explained, and while doing so encountered British packets right in the middle of the stream battling to make headway. The whalers would hail the British ships, Folger said, and tell them they were "stemming a current that was against them to the value of three miles an hour," but, alas, "they were too wise to be counselled by simple American fisherman." Their stubbornness, he added, cost them as much as 70 miles a day, and, when propelling winds were not strong enough, the current might even have driven the English ships backwards.

Ever the scientist, Franklin asked his cousin to trace out the current for him and had it engraved, but the captains of the Falmouth mail packets apparently paid little heed when the Franklin-Folger chart appeared in 1769 or 1770. That was unfortunate; for its time, this first formalized recognition of the Gulf Stream was remarkably accurate. And the copy Franklin gave to the French a few years later may well have helped their ships speed aid to the rebellious colonies.

Though initially snubbed by English sailors, the Gulf Stream has become the most thoroughly studied current in the oceans. And for good reason: It is a stream of superlatives, peaking at velocities of more than nine knots in its narrowest corridor between Florida and the Bahamas and carrying up to 90 million cubic meters of water every second—enough to fill 90 million king-sized bathtubs—as it passes near Chesapeake Bay. And of history: The Spaniards, who discovered the current in the 16th Century (but kept its whereabouts a state secret), sent their gold-laden galleons homeward bound on its swift waters, the *Carrera de Indias* ("Highway of the Indies"), as they called them.

The Gulf Stream has also spawned myths, the most the beguiling that its warm waters flow all the way to the British Isles and account for their balmy climate, though they sit at the latitude of Labrador. The chilblained truth is, as recent investigations indicate, that Britain's relatively mild winters are only indirectly the result of the Gulf Stream, which transports warm water to relatively high latitudes. From there, winds carry the warmth to Britain and Europe. Still, without the tools of modern oceanography, early students of the stream can be forgiven for overstating its effects. To the mariner riding the current (or battling against it), the Gulf Stream is an awesome natural force, a heat machine that would have to burn five billion tons of coal an hour if one tried to match its energy output. The U.S. Navy's pioneering oceanographer, Lieutenant Matthew Fontaine Maury, in his 1855 classic *The Physical Geography of the Sea*, immortalized it forever with these lyrical lines: "There is a river in the ocean. In the severest droughts it never fails, and in the mightiest floods it never overflows. Its banks and its bottoms are of cold water, while its current is of warm. The Gulf of Mexico is its fountain, and its mouth is in the Arctic Seas. It is the Gulf Stream."

But Maury was wrong. The stream is not a single riverine current as steady as the Mississippi, nor is it born in the Gulf of Mexico; it is part of a vastly more complex system of flows that crisscross much of the North Atlantic. The first inkling of its intricacy came as a result of an unlikely patron's curiosity. Tired of idle pleasure cruises on his yacht *Hirondelle*, the young Prince Albert I of Monaco decided to use some of his family's wealth from the gaming tables of Monte Carlo to learn more about the sea. In 1885, with the help of a mentor, Professor Georges Pouchet of the Paris Museum of Natural History, he began investigating ocean currents by setting afloat from his yacht 150 glass bottles, 10 copper spheres and 20 beer barrels, each containing instructions in 10 languages asking finders to write the prince about the time and place of their discovery.

On subsequent cruises, the prince and the professor released hundreds more bottles and barrels, and eventually received reports on 227. By plotting their drift, the two investigators concluded that the Gulf Stream breaks up in the northeastern Atlantic just beyond the Grand Banks—part of it heading farther northeast past the British Isles and Scandinavia, part of it veering southeast along southern Europe

Transporting warm water from the straits between Florida and the Bahamas, the Gulf Stream stretches to the east just north of Cape Hatteras as a yellow filament in this heat-sensing satellite image. (Magenta is the coldest water—32° F—and yellow is the warmest—77° F.) The current carries a hundred times the water flow of all the world's rivers combined and helps transport equatorial heat to the North Atlantic, spawning westerly winds that warm the British Isles.

and Africa. Then they made an even more astonishing discovery: Since two of the objects Albert released off France were recovered in the West Indies, it was clear that the southeasterly flow eventually turned west and recrossed the Atlantic as part of the North Equatorial Current—the same current that took Columbus to the New World. The Gulf Stream was thus only one leg of a great gyre, or whirl, of water circling the North Atlantic in a clockwise flow.

Today, scientists using more sophisticated instruments have mapped gyres and currents with unparalleled accuracy. One of the more successful tools used by oceanographers is the Acoustic Doppler Current Profiler, a state-of-the-art instrument that works by sending out a beam of sound at a fixed frequency and listening for its faint echoes scattered off particles in the water. (Sound, as noisy cetaceans learned long ago, is the a far better probe than sight since water at any depth is largely opaque to sunlight.) As the device's name indicates, it depends on the Doppler effect, the familiar shift in frequency, or pitch, of sound waves that occurs, for example, when a whistling train sweeps by: The pitch becomes increasingly higher as the train approaches, lower as it recedes into the distance. By looking for such changes in the backscattered sound, the instrument can tell how fast the water is moving and in what direction. But that is only part of its versatility: Broadcasting beams in a number of directions and treating the echoes as separate "cells"—for volumes of water—the computerized device can simultaneously measure water velocities at various depths. Even a single profiler, moored at sea or lowered from a ship, can do the work of a whole string of simpler current meters.

Even more ingenious are free-floating instruments that drift under the sea at predetermined depths and tip off their whereabouts by the sounds they broadcast. They are acronymically named SOFAR floats, after what scientists call the ocean's "sound fixing and ranging" channel—a kind of megaphone in the sea at a depth of a half mile to a mile that transmits sound with exceptional efficiency. Whales, for instance, can send their "songs" over distances of a thousand miles or more though this channel. By listening to a float's pinging over a period of time at several scattered stations simultaneously, and using the telltale sounds to triangulate its various positions, modern oceanographers can plot hidden undersea currents with unequaled precision.

Still, SOFAR floats have two drawbacks. They do not operate well at great depths and they are expensive. In a clever flipflop of function, University of Rhode Island oceanographer H. Thomas Rossby and his colleagues developed a new instrument called a RAFOS (SOFAR backwards) float. While the original devices broadcast their position to an array of underwater listening stations, RAFOS drifters simply record incoming sounds from the moored stations, along with temperature and density readings. That means most of the fancy electronics are in the stations, which are few in number, rather than in the numerous floats, so the experimenting becomes much cheaper. At the end of their tours, usually about 45 days, RAFOS drifters shed their ballast, pop to the surface and "upload" their data to a passing satellite that relays the information from the deep to shore-based oceanographers. Prince Albert, patiently waiting for mailed information on his recovered bottles, would surely have marveled at such speedy ocean science.

THE TALE OF THE RINGS

A satellite photograph of the Gulf Stream that distinguishes warm from cooler waters by computer-imposed colors, does not show the clear, sharply defined "river in the ocean" of the Franklin-Folger chart, but a jumble of loops and whirls—visible on the photograph on page 37. Resembling the fiery breath of a Chinese dragon, the eddies seem to be breaking away from the main body of water, spinning off with whatever oceanic life might be trapped inside them.

Over the years, sailors riding the Gulf Stream undoubtedly noticed the strange eddies, but no one paid them much heed until the 1930s when scientists at the newly established Woods Hole Oceanographic Institution, on Cape Cod, started getting inquisitive. Among them was the oceanographer-yachtsman Columbus O'Donnell Iselin, one of the institution's founding fathers who, living up to his name, had been sailing Gulf Stream waters off Cape Cod since his youth. On the eve of World War II, he published what was apparently the first scientific paper on the eddies, which implicated them in a lingering biological puzzle—the periodic deaths of shallow-water creatures that were mysteriously swept out into the inhospitable open sea. But what caused the eddies—and what their role was in

EARS ACROSS THE WATER

For most people, listening to the ocean is to be enchanted by its sounds. But, for oceanographers, "an ear to the sea" means gathering practical information about the nature of the oceans. Sound waves are at the heart of Ocean Acoustic Tomography, a system developed in 1977 to measure the speed, direction and size of currents, and the wide range of ocean temperatures.

Ocean Acoustic Tomography relies on instruments that both transmit and receive sound. Operating around the perimeter of a body of water, a few dozen of these transceivers crisscross the expanse (which could be as vast as an ocean basin) by establishing pathways made up of sound waves. The behavior of a signal is affected by the nature of the water through which it travels. Sound travels about five times faster through water than air —roughly one mile per second. Moreover, its velocity is quickened or slowed by water temperature, pressure, salinity and current speeds. Oceanogaphers, who know what route a specific ray of sound has traveled, can interpret the changes in travel time; when pooled, the information reveals a vast, three-dimensional profile of the water. The process is similar to the computerized axial tomography (CAT) scans, which use X-rays to produce three-dimensional images of the brain.

Even precise maps of the Gulf Stream in the North Atlantic have been drawn using acoustic tomography. Currently, it takes a few months to retrieve and analyze the data, but oceanographers hope the Ocean Acoustic Tomography system eventually will be improved to provide quicker results. Floating beacons, tethered to the moorings, will transmit the data instantaneously by satellite, providing oceanographers with an immediate picture of the ocean's interior.

A WEB OF SOUND WAVES

An array of ocean acoustic tomography moorings three miles deep is used to measure ocean temperatures, pressure and currents over an area of 150 miles square. The web of sound waves that extends between the moorings helps oceanographers develop a three-dimensional image of a vast area and volume of ocean.

Locator

A strobe light and radio allow easy location of the Ocean Acoustic Tomography moorings. The transceivers must be manually retrieved and the stored data interpreted, a process that can take several months.

Transponder

Three transponders surround each anchor in an equilateral triangle and transmit a signal to the transceiver in response to an acoustic signal. By measuring the travel time, the transponders help measure the sway of the moorings with an accuracy of three feet.

Transceiver

Located at a depth of slightly less than a mile, a transceiver both sends out and receives sound signals at a predetermined frequency, communicating with instruments at other moorings.

Hydrophone

The devices "listen" to waterborne sound waves; the information is then stored by the transceivers.

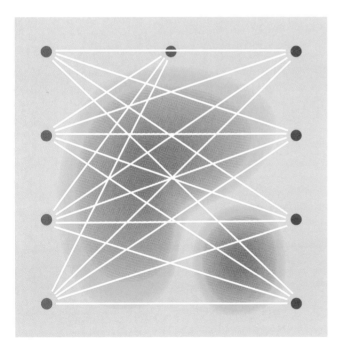

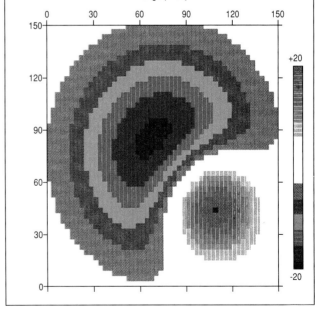

A Thermal Sounding

In this simulation of ocean acoustic tomography, nine transceivers that transmit and receive acoustic signals are moored to the ocean floor around a 150-mile square area of water *(left)*. Temperature readings are determined by transmitting sound signals in a crisscrossing pattern between the transceivers and timing their speed. (Sound travels faster in warmer water than cold.) After processing the data with a computer, circular regions of warm and cold water are revealed in the image at right. It shows that sound speed at a depth of 650 feet ranged from -20 feet per second to +20 feet per second above the standard speed of sound in 55°F water—5,000 feet per second.

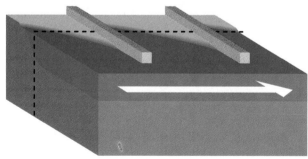

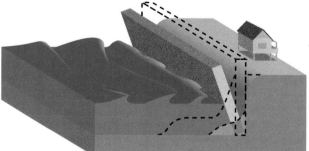

TRYING TO STEM EROSION'S RELENTLESS FORCE

Short structures that extend out from shore called groins (above) are designed to reduce the impact of waves and capture the sand that moves along in longshore currents. Unfortunately, sand only builds up on the down-current side of the groin, while erosion takes place on the other.

Built to protect oceanfront property from the natural erosion of beaches and shorelines, seawalls often deflect wave energy onto the sand in front of the seawall, which contributes to erosion. As well, when the ocean's forces destroy a seawall the property and beach become particularly vulnerable.

Threatened Beaches

Beaches are dynamic formations; the forces of wind, waves and tides that create them continuously redistribute littoral sands and gravels. These forces also establish barrier islands, the frontline of defense against the relentless ocean. Lying just offshore, these ribbons of sand, with their delicate dunes and vegetation, are popular holiday home locations. Unfortunately, beaches and barrier islands are particularly fragile and poorly equipped to withstand intensive use.

Erosion is a natural phenomenon along coastlines; beaches disappear without any human help. But recently they have been retreating at a disturbing rate: Monterey Beach, in California, recedes 5 to 15 feet annually; high water at Long Island, New York, is 100 feet farther inland than it was 50 years ago; and along the 530 miles of France's east coast a yard is lost every year. Rising ocean levels are part of the problem. But there are other causes. Busy ports alter the currents that naturally transport sand; beachside construction often involves the destruction of protective dunes; and sunseekers frequently trample the vegetation that stabilizes the backside of beaches.

Efforts to prevent the beaches' retreat largely have been unsuccessful. Structures that imitate protective barrier islands and reefs are expensive and only moderately effective. The most effective technique, known as beach nourishment, involves dumping fresh sand along the retreating shore to replace the disappearing sediments.

Beach erosion cannot be stopped; at best it can be slowed. The most sensible plan is to build back farther from the sandy shores or to shield the most delicate beach environments from overuse. But eventually, beachlovers may have to concede that protecting beaches is more important than protecting the property on them.

Houses built on piles driven into the sand, such as these on Long Island, New York, are vulnerable when the beach erodes under the natural forces of winds, waves and tides.

the broader world of oceanic circulation—was still unknown. These issues did not come under serious study until after the war when another colorful Woods Hole scientist, Frederick C. Fuglister, an artist turned oceanographer, succeeded in identifying an eddy that had separated from the Gulf Stream and proceeded in almost the opposite direction, revolving like a miniature ocean gyre. Since then eddies—or rings, their more popular name—have been found to be a prominent feature of almost all strong ocean currents, including the Kuroshio in the Pacific and the Agulhas Current off the southern tip of Africa, site of the largest, most energetic rings yet measured.

Some scientists consider the tornado-like eddies storms in the sea. But what causes these storms remains imperfectly understood, though scientists have done much in recent years to clarify matters by their intensive exploration of the Gulf Stream. As its warm waters spread out into the Atlantic off Cape Hatteras, they have found, it brushes up against the cold, southerly flowing Labrador Current from the Arctic. Whether or not this close encounter is to blame, the Gulf Stream begins to meander, forming loops or bends, like rivers do on land. Some of these bends grow so big that they eventually bud off from the main current and, like an oxbow lake, begin a life of their own.

Unlike the sluggish lake, however, the ring spins vigorously. It is a bit of Gulf Stream moving around upon itself, with a core of calm water trapped in its midst. Rings pinched off the north side of the stream whirl in a clockwise direction at a speed of two or three knots and tend to drift to the southwest. Such breakaway eddies are called warm-core rings because they entrap warm water from the Sargasso Sea. The heated, encircled water at the center of the ring is so buoyant that it rises to levels a foot or more above the surrounding sea.

On the southern side of the stream, the rings are born with a counterclockwise spin. Wrapped around a core of cold, dense northern water, they tend to sink in the middle slightly below the level of the surrounding sea. Up to 200 miles in diameter, these cold-core rings, as they are called, are about half again as large as their warm-core kin and may extend all the way to the bottom of the sea floor. They also survive longer, from an average of 18 months to as much as three years, before being reabsorbed by the Gulf Stream.

In 1977 oceanographer Philip L. Richardson and colleagues from Woods Hole, following in the wake of Fuglister's innovative work on the eddies, became the first witnesses to the complete life cycle of a ring, albeit a relatively short-lived one. In February they saw the beginnings of a large meander in the Gulf Stream. In March they observed the loop break off as a cold-core eddy and dubbed it Ring Bob. In April the ring reattached itself to the Gulf Stream, only to spin off on its own again in May. Ring Bob remained free until September, when it was reabsorbed by the Gulf Stream off Chesapeake Bay and its rotating motion slowly dissipated in the flow of its parent current. (Shortly thereafter, Richardson capped

1

2

THE BIRTH OF A RING

A gigantic whirlpool known as a ring, which spins at an average of two miles per hour with a core of quiet water imprisoned in the middle, begins when a meander forms in a current—in this case, the Gulf Stream (1). The loop tightens and draws cold, nutrient-rich water into a pocket in the warm Sargasso Sea (2). Later it closes completely, trapping a core of cold water within a swirling ring of warm Gulf Stream water. The movement of the warm water imparts a counterclockwise spin to the ring (3). Finally, the ring breaks free and begins its life as an independent current (4). (A similar ring can be seen east of North Carolina's Cape Hatteras in the satellite photo on page 37.) Rings accompany most strong ocean currents and can spin both in clockwise and counterclockwise directions. Some can last for several years before being absorbed by the surrounding sea.

his triumph at sea by rediscovering a lost version of the old Franklin-Folger Gulf Stream chart in a Paris archive.)

Predicting the formation of rings, or anticipating their future behavior, remains something of an art, like weather forecasting. But it is being done by teams using powerful computers at Harvard University, and at the National Oceanic and Atmospheric Administration, which issues five-times-a-week satellite-based charts of Gulf Stream activity. And the results are eagerly anticipated—by fishermen looking for prize catches such as the tuna known to lurk at the edges of rings, by pollution fighters wondering how the sea will disperse an oil spill and by racing yachtsmen eager to get an extra boost past a rival from an eddy's current. Yet while scientists are honing their skills at gulfcasting, as they call it, oceanography is still aswirl with questions about the eddies, such as why cold-core rings are generally larger than warm-core rings and why the former last longer.

3

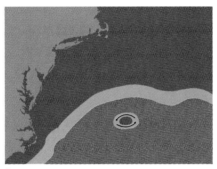

4

Geography almost certainly plays some role. Squeezed between the continental shelf and the Gulf Stream, the inshore warm-core eddies may have less room to maneuver before they are caught up again in the clutches of their parent current. Biologists, for their part, have questions too. As a ring moves away from a major current, it carries off countless marine animals and plants, sometimes stranding them in a watery grave, such as the hot, barren Sargasso Sea. How such mass movements figure in the health of marine populations and whether they stimulate evolutionary change remain mysteries.

Whatever the answers, the importance of the rings is undoubtedly deep—in a very real sense. For some years, scientists have been puzzled by a strange phenomenon they call abyssal storms. These are unexpected bursts of current that sweep abruptly across the sea floor, raising great clouds of sediment in areas once thought to be serenely free of disturbance. Woods Hole oceanographer Charles Hollister, who in more than a decade of studying the storms has found his instruments repeatedly bowled over by them, likens them to blizzards on land. It is not a farfetched comparison, even though these bottom currents are tortoise-slow. Because the ocean is a thousand times as dense as the atmosphere, a typical current of only a knot at a depth of three miles can pack the wallop of a 35-mile-an-hour gale. These rings may fan submarine winds.

Certainly, there are strong indications that the eddies create powerful and unpredictable currents in the deep sea. Before the United States established a 200-mile fishing zone off its coast in 1976, New England lobstermen regularly complained that offshore Soviet fishing fleets were destroying or removing their traps. Yet lobster pots continued to vanish, or float off many miles, even after the foreign fleets had left the scene, so American fishermen were forced to admit that powerful currents were at work on the sea floor. More recently, oceanographer George Weatherly and his associates at Florida State University linked the eddies to the sea floor upheavals directly. By methodically matching satellite observations of rings with current measurements on the bottom, they were able to establish an undeniable connection between the formation of specific eddies on the surface and the occurrence of abyssal storms.

These findings surprised many oceanographers, who have long felt that the sea could not transmit such mechanical forces vertically through so many layers. But, as Hollister explains, the action is similar to what happens when you stir tea in a cup. Even if your spoon goes only halfway down, the force of the stirring will eventually be felt by a leaf on the bottom and it will begin to move. "The ocean," he adds, "is much stiffer than we ever imagined."

THE DESTRUCTIVE IMPACT OF EL NIÑO

Nurtured by cool, nutrient-rich upwellings from the floor of the continental shelf, the waters off Peru are among the most fertile in the world. They throb with anchovies, the tiny, herringlike fish that feast on the greenish-brown pastures of phytoplankton flourishing in these waters. For years the little fish have ensured Peru's well-being. In 1970, during their industry's heyday, Peru's *bolicheras* (draggers) hauled in 13 million tons of anchovies, a fifth of the world's total fish catch.

But periodically this bonanza from the sea comes a cropper when a warm equatorial current—for reasons still hotly debated by scientists—begins to wash the shore. It blocks the rich, organically laden nutrients from rising from the sea floor, which, in turn, support the phytoplankton; soon, the anchoveta are all but gone. In the heat brought by the tropical waters, the coastal sea plankton and other marine life die. Sea birds starve for lack of food, and with them goes another valuable resource, guano—bird droppings loaded with nitrogen and phosphorus that make splendid fertilizer.

All too often the feverish waters have been an unwelcome gift around Christmas time, prompting 19th-Century Peruvian fishermen to call them *El Niño*, Spanish for The [Christ] Child. (These episodes were not universally deplored. If there was no serious flooding, farmers welcomed the heavy seasonal rains that accompanied El Niño and that turned their normally arid fields into lush pastureland. They call such good times *años de abundancia*, or years of abundance.) No one knows how long El Niños have been wreaking ecological and economic havoc on Peru and Ecuador, though old weather logs describe such conditions as long ago as the early 1700s. But by far the worst El Niño in a century took place in the winter of 1982-1983. The fish catch dwindled to barely a quarter of what it had been in the previous year and torrential rains—up to 11 feet in areas that usually get about six inches—unleashed huge landslides and floods, leaving 600 people dead, thousands homeless and billions of dollars in damage.

Yet as severe as the suffering was in Peru and Ecuador, meteorological disaster befell other countries as well. Australia, experiencing its worst drought in at least a century, turned into a virtual dustbowl. Brush fires erupted everywhere, desperate kangaroos invaded farms for water, and topsoil whipped up into giant dust storms; one great cloud appeared over Melbourne on February 8 and suddenly turned a sunny afternoon into darkest night, stirring fears of the end of the world. Killing droughts also gripped Indonesia, the Philippines, India and Sri Lanka, as well as Botswana, in southeastern Africa. By contrast, the South Pacific island of Tahiti, untouched by hurricanes in this century, was drenched by six devastating tropical

EL NIÑO'S SHIFTING WEATHER PATTERNS
Periodically, the phenomenon known as El Niño creates massive, global fluctuation in normal weather patterns. The changes are the result of the shifting of a low-pressure system in the South Pacific, which alters the trade winds that, in turn, affect the flow of surface currents. The result—along with the disruption of the normal upwelling of nutrients in the eastern South Pacific—is a dislocation of climate patterns felt all the way from America to Australia.

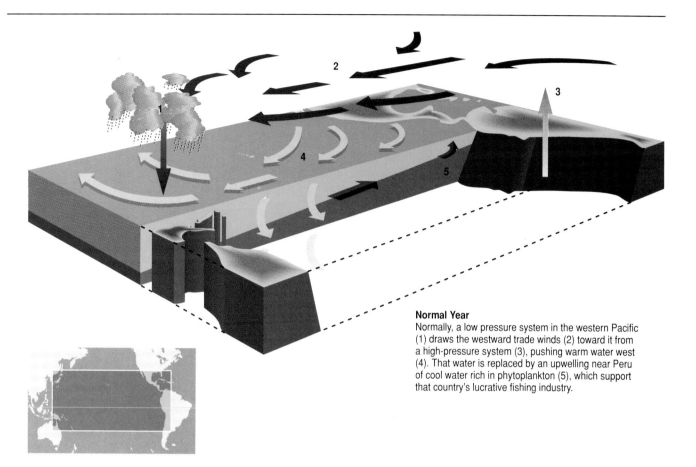

Normal Year
Normally, a low pressure system in the western Pacific
(1) draws the westward trade winds (2) toward it from
a high-pressure system (3), pushing warm water west
(4). That water is replaced by an upwelling near Peru
of cool water rich in phytoplankton (5), which support
that country's lucrative fishing industry.

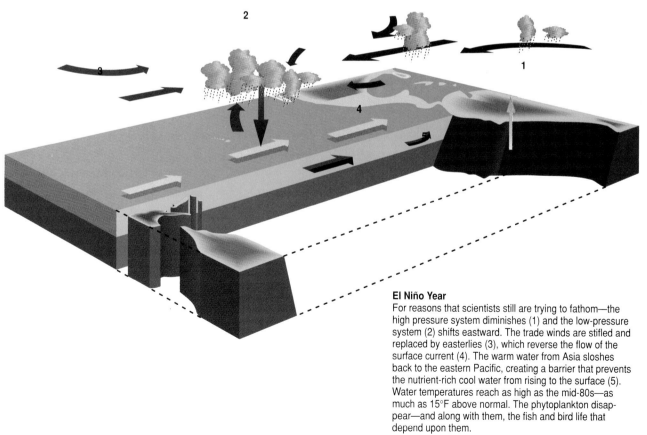

El Niño Year
For reasons that scientists still are trying to fathom—the
high pressure system diminishes (1) and the low-pressure
system (2) shifts eastward. The trade winds are stifled and
replaced by easterlies (3), which reverse the flow of the
surface current (4). The warm water from Asia sloshes
back to the eastern Pacific, creating a barrier that prevents
the nutrient-rich cool water from rising to the surface (5).
Water temperatures reach as high as the mid-80s—as
much as 15°F above normal. The phytoplankton disappear—and along with them, the fish and bird life that
depend upon them.

storms in only five months, while in the United States, the California and Gulf coasts were lashed by extraordinary winds, waves and rains that caused millions of dollars in losses.

If scientists ever suspected that El Niño was more than just a meteorological quirk of Peru and Ecuador, the freakish worldwide weather of late 1982 and the early months of 1983 convinced them. As the simultaneous events indicated, the stifling waters and biblical rains in South America were clearly linked to major changes in currents, winds and atmospheric pressure many thousands of miles away. And for scientists that was a silver lining: Never before had they had such a textbook example of how intimately the oceans and atmosphere are entwined. Probing every aspect of the events, they set out to understand them, and perhaps even learn to predict them.

At first glance, one would be hard put to link a change in the waters off South America with meteorological mayhem elsewhere in the world. But an initial hint of a possible connection was uncovered in the 1920s by the British mathematician Gilbert Walker, director general of the colonial weather service in India. Something of a polymath who was interested in everything from birds to boomerangs, Walker became intrigued by India's monsoons, the stiff summer winds that bring the nourishing rains so vital to the country, yet which so often fail. Studying meteorological records from around the world in an effort to determine whether the monsoon is part of some global weather pattern, Walter found a curious correlation between two widely separated events:

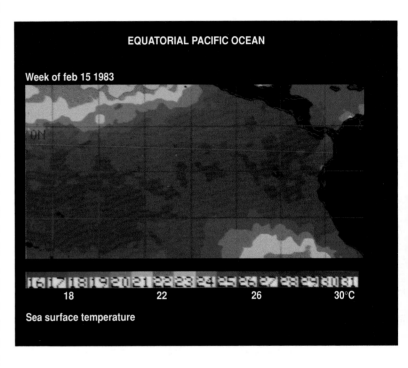

When barometric pressures are higher than normal over the South Pacific, they tend to be lower than normal over the Indian Ocean, and the usual winds and rains appear. Every few years, however, the pattern reverses. Low pressure over the Pacific is accompanied by high pressure over the Indian Ocean and that means drought. Walker called this meteorological seesaw the Southern Oscillation.

Walker, who received a knighthood for his investigations of monsoons, never connected the oscillation with El Niño nor did he find a reliable way to predict the annual rains, but his work produced a striking insight: It suggested that climatic perturbations in one part of the world would inevitably be felt elsewhere. In retrospect this idea may seem patently obvious, but it was ignored until 1958—coincidentally, the year of Walker's death at age 90—when a rare scientific opportunity presented itself: El Niño reappeared just as scientists from 66 nations were embarking on the largest study ever undertaken of Earth and nearby space, the International Geophysical Year. Their myriad instruments in place, scientists went to work on El Niño with unmatched intensity.

Out of the mother lode of data collected during this year of Earth science, the American meteorologist Jacob Aall Bjerknes not only firmly established the link between El Niño and the Southern Oscillation, but also explained how they reinforced one another. During a Southern Oscillation, the prevailing westerly Pacific

During the disastrous El Niño of 1982-1983, warm water from the western Pacific pushed all the way to the South American coast, as seen in the satellite photo above, preventing cool water from reaching the surface and replenishing the nutrients necessary to sustain oceanic life. By November 1983, the weather conditions that produced El Niño had reversed (right) and a tongue of cool water is visible stretching west into the Pacific.

trade winds first increase (a transitory state of affairs scientists now whimsically feminize as La Niña), then they diminish in strength. As the trades taper off, or even reverse direction, the warm equatorial water they have been propelling westward suddenly starts sloshing back toward South America. Approaching the coast, the countercurrent blocks the cold Humboldt Current as it courses up from the south, disrupts the fertile upwellings and covers the entire region with heavy humid air, all classic characteristics of El Niño. Meanwhile, across the Pacific, the great, soggy mass of warm air that usually drapes Australia and Indonesia because of the prevailing east-to-west tropical winds is replaced by dry, cool air. Rainfall becomes precious or nonexistent. Though these events occur on opposite sides of the great ocean, they are so intimately related that scientists nowadays speak of them as one: El Niño/Southern Oscillation.

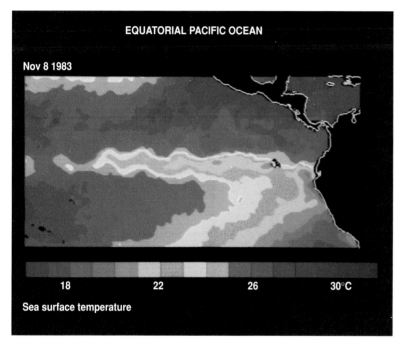

EQUATORIAL PACIFIC OCEAN

Nov 8 1983

18   22   26   30°C

Sea surface temperature

Beyond showing the underlying linkage between two puzzling phenomena, Bjerknes finally got the scientific community to recognize what he called "teleconnections"—the influence of one part of the oceans or atmosphere on other parts. Or as University of Maryland climate analyst Eugene Rasmussen put it: "When one part of the atmosphere moves, another part feels the kick."

Yet as sharp as those kicks may be, scientists are still unsure what provokes them. They wonder why, for example, trade winds falter in the first place. In 1969, after collecting still more data, Bjerknes concluded that the Southern Oscillation is preceded by a rise in sea-surface temperatures in the tropical Pacific. These in turn heat the air overhead and interfere with the prevailing winds. But no one is sure what causes the heating. Over the years, various investigators have implicated everything from sunspots to volcanic eruptions to planetary alignments, all of which can upset Earth's heat balance. One scientist has even linked the higher water temperatures to increased earthquake activity along the East Pacific Rise, a rift valley on the sea floor where the emergence of hot molten lava from deep within Earth creates new crustal material. But critics wonder how heat released at 8,000 feet can surface quickly enough to provide the required warming.

Perhaps the most widely accepted explanation is in a sense the most unexpected. Based on their computer modeling of the events that must occur to produce El Niño/Southern Oscillation, scientists now are saying that it is simply one phase of a repeating natural cycle. By this reasoning, it is not externally caused but the result of a continuous interplay of atmosphere and ocean. Warm water accumulates in the equatorial Pacific before El Niño, yet even as it begins lapping against South America, it is already setting the stage for the appearance of cooler water that will spell the episode's end and the start of still another repetition of the cycle. Only the disruptive effects of random disturbances, say the modelers, who have been working on ways to forecast El Niños, keep Walker's old transpacific seesaw from being as regular as the seasons—or as predictable.

A TREASURE TROVE OF LIFE

I n February 1977, a seemingly routine research voyage turned into a biologist's dream come true. Cruising one-and-a-half miles below the surface of the South Pacific northeast of the Galápagos Islands in a three-passenger submarine named *Alvin*, marine scientists John B. Corliss and John M. Edmond peered through tiny plexiglass portholes, searching for some curious-looking foot-long white clams recently photographed on the ocean floor by a deep-towed photographic sled that had happened to pass over them. As the pilot steered the craft slowly above the ocean floor's bleak, slate-gray terrain, *Alvin*'s headlamps pierced the inky blackness revealing little life. A pair of purple sea anemones, their tentacles waiting for tiny carcasses to drift down from above, broke the monotony of yard upon yard of lifeless, moon-like landscape.

But then Corliss and Edmond were struck by something peculiar about the water. It shimmered, in Edmond's words, "like the air above hot pavement." Intrigued, the pilot guided the 16.5-ton *Alvin* up a shallow slope. The scene that next met their eyes was one that neither scientist would ever forget, a tableau that would turn one of biology's most treasured tenets inside out.

Every biologist yearns to discover new organisms. Corliss and Edmond had discovered not just the strange white clams, but a whole community of animals, including six-foot-long tube worms and vast fields of yellow mussels, which were thriving where no biologist had ever thought a community could survive—in a completely lightless environment.

Warm water streamed from cracks in the seafloor over a circular area 100 yards wide. The shimmering water seemed to support the community; beyond the warm zone, the number of creatures declined dramatically. Using the *Alvin*'s robotic arm to snatch a few specimens, the scientists gathered all the data they could, before returning to the surface. Later, laboratory analysis showed that the deep-vent community derived its sustenance from a novel form of food production called chemosynthesis. Somehow the creatures were able to derive energy from gas in

The coral reefs of the Red Sea harbor a miraculous variety of creatures—some of the more than 200,000 species that inhabit the salt water realm. Of all life on Earth, nearly 80 percent is to be found in the oceans.

the water—rather than from sunlight—and use that energy to produce the necessary carbohydrates to sustain life.

Corliss' and Edmond's find—later dubbed Rose Garden—was one of the most dramatic discoveries of 20th Century marine biology. But it was far from being an isolated surprise. In probing the ocean, from the shoreline to the abyss, scientists have steadily uncovered the mysteries of how life in the oceans exists—and co-exists—from microscopic organisms to 100-ton whales. And with that fresh understanding has come a new appreciation of the intricate connectiveness of all the vastly varied creatures that occupy the ocean domain, a realm containing 250 times more living space than the one humans occupy on land.

LIVING OFF THE SUN

The most unusual aspect of Rose Garden was not the profusion of yellow, pink and red organisms, mostly unknown to science. The real surprise was the color Corliss and Edmond did not find: green. Formerly, scientists had believed that the profusion of life in the oceans—indeed all life on Earth—survived because of a single biological process called photosynthesis, in which a bright-green chemical called chlorophyll captures energy from the Sun and links carbon atoms to make sugars. Photosynthesis, scientists thought, makes the biological world go round.

Many organisms photosynthesize. Green plants and pond-scum algae do it on land. Myriad marine algae—from free-floating single cells to kelp, a seaweed that can grow hundreds of feet long—photosynthesize in the sea. And bluish-green photosynthetic bacteria called cyanobacteria carry on the process on both land and sea, inhabiting nearly every environment on Earth.

In oceans all over the world, the top few hundred yards of water—known as the sunlit zone—swarm with tiny organisms, drawn near the surface by the Sun's life-sustaining light. Because they float passively on the currents or swim only weakly, biologists call them plankton, from *planktos*, the Greek word for drifting. The term encompasses two principal groups: phytoplankton—plantlike photosynthetic organisms, including single-celled algae; and zooplankton—animal-like organisms such as tiny fish, shrimp and jellyfish. The former are producers, clustered near the surface because most water below a few hundred yards transmits too little light for efficient photosynthesis; the latter are the consumers who feed on the producers. Together, they form the base of a food chain that encompasses the diverse creatures that live in the ocean. Tiny consumers eat producers, larger animals eat the eaters and so on. In this watery jungle, the dictum is eat or be eaten.

The pyramid-like structure of the food web, with the phytoplankton at the bottom and the largest fish and mammals at the top, means that only a small portion of the food value is transferred at each step. Each time one animal eats another 80 to 90 percent of the energy escapes as heat and waste. One hundred pounds of phytoplankton will support 10 pounds of the tiny crustacean krill. That 10 pounds, in turn, will support only one pound of fish. With all this energy loss, animals stand to gain a great deal by short-circuiting the food chain. The great baleen whales—some grow to 100 feet long and weigh 100 tons—skip numerous steps, devouring schools of krill and small fish in a single gulp. A daily whale diet may total more than two million calories, three tons of krill. Other large marine animals also eat low on the food chain, including giant manta rays and whale sharks, at

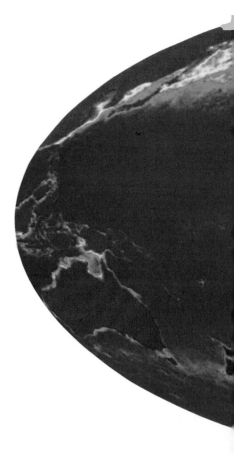

Viewed from a Nimbus 7 research satellite, the oceans of the world reveal variations in their chlorophyll content. The pigment is central to the process of photosynthesis, by which tiny, plantlike creatures in the ocean produce the carbohydrates that sustain life. The higher the chlorophyll content the greater the biological activity in the water and therefore the greater the concentration of marine life.

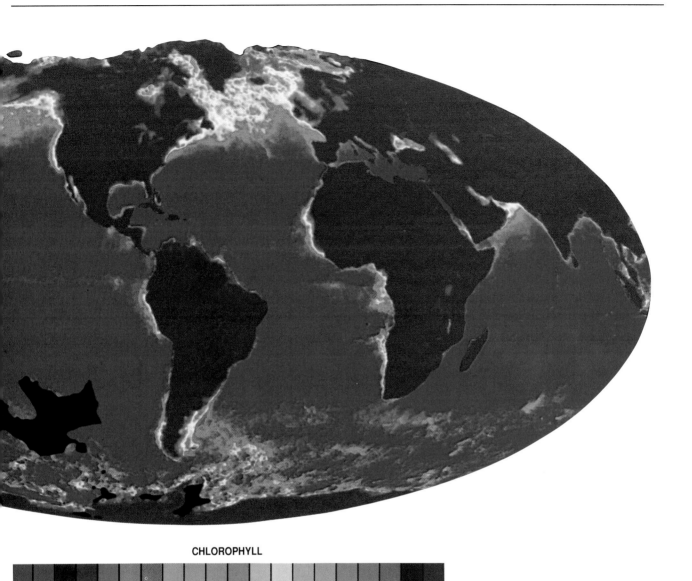

CHLOROPHYLL

Less   More

60 feet long, the world's largest fish. Many smaller fish, such as herring, menhaden, anchovies, sardines and mackerel also consume plankton.

Phytoplankton, including some cyanobacteria, produce nearly 90 percent of all the food in the ocean. In certain local ecosystems, fast-growing giant seaweeds may rival phytoplankton in food production. But for sheer numbers the world over—as many as 12 million per cubic foot of water—phytoplankton win hands down. They produce perhaps two-thirds of all the food on Earth—as much as 160 billion tons per year. And making all this food production possible is the Sun's energy, streaming onto the Earth in packets of light called photons.

Of all the millions of photons striking the planet (hundreds of trillions hit Earth every second, but most are reflected or absorbed and converted into heat) only a minuscule fraction contributes to photosynthesis. It is this infinitesimal amount that makes life on Earth—and in the oceans—possible. In photosynthesis, photons impacting chlorophyll trigger chemical reactions that store energy. This chemical energy can then be used to link the carbon atoms from carbon dioxide (CO_2) to

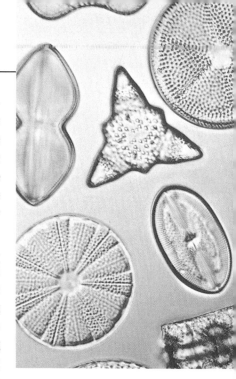

the hydrogens and oxygen from water (H$_2$O), forming simple sugars such as glucose (C$_6$H$_{12}$O$_6$), which provides sustenance. In this photosynthetic reaction, oxygen is left over, escaping as gas (O$_2$). Oxygen-producing photosynthesis, the only source of oxygen in Earth's atmosphere, began about three billion years ago, a billion years after the planet coalesced out of a primordial cloud of gas. Early primitive cells photosynthesized using relatively rare chemicals instead of water, and some bacteria continue that tradition today, but the ability to use ubiquitous water allowed the modern photosynthesizers to flourish.

With the production of oxygen, the Earth's early atmosphere began to change. Some bacteria—the only organisms yet in existence—died off, but others survived and developed. During this evolution, a remarkable event seems to have taken place. A large consumer cell engulfed a small photosynthetic one. Instead of being digested, this small cell merely continued photosynthesizing, absorbing wastes and releasing sugar and oxygen. These early photosynthetic roomers, according to the endosymbiotic hypothesis (from two Greek words meaning inside and living together), evolved into chloroplasts, the chlorophyll-containing photosynthetic part of today's plants and algae. Such an association may seem farfetched, but many such endosymbiotic relationships—often between animals and algae—are found in the sea, greatly enriching certain habitats.

OF DIATOMS AND DINOFLAGELLATES

Phytoplankton have evolved exquisite adaptations to their wandering existence. Planktonic eggs contain minute drops of oil that improve buoyancy. When the larvae hatch they consume the yolk sac and are buoyed up by the oil. Diatoms—the most abundant and productive phytoplankton in many rich areas—secrete delicate glassy shells in two halves that fit together like a pill box. A single scoop of seawater may contain thousands of diatoms, each only four one-thousandths of an inch in diameter. They store food from photosynthesis as oil, a long-lasting food reserve. In addition, some diatom shells include long filaments, which act like anchors to slow their descent. Dead diatoms sink to the bottom, their shells accumulating and condensing in layers thousands of feet thick.

Second only to diatoms in numbers and production is a varied group called the dinoflagellates. Some dinoflagellates photosynthesize, others lack chlorophyll and live as parasites or carnivores. Some photosynthetic dinoflagellates live within the cells of sea anemones and coral animals as endosymbionts, adding yet another layer to the endosymbiotic relationship they enjoy with their own chloroplasts.

Photosynthetic dinoflagellates so successfully exploit good growing conditions that their populations occasionally explode. Under certain conditions and in certain places, cold, deep seawater laden with nutrients wells up to the surface. This added fertilizer, combined with sunny weather, creates ideal growing conditions, pushing dinoflagellates to a million times their normal population. In such conditions, a quart of seawater can contain 100 million dinoflagellates. Such a "bloom" can result in a tide red with dinoflagellate pigments. (Marine algae occasionally produce blooms of other colors—brown and green, for example—depending on the color of their chloroplasts.)

Red tides can be disastrous. The particular strains of dinoflagellates that produce them manufacture a toxin that kills thousands of tons of fish during a single bloom.

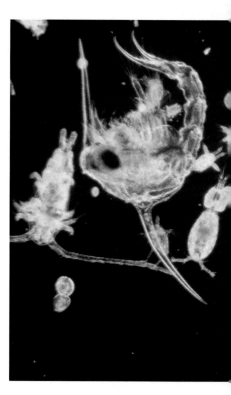

Life in the oceans ultimately depends on tiny plants and algae known as phytoplankton (top). Using the sun's life-giving powers, the microscopic organisms create the basic foodstuff that feed the next level of life: the zooplankton (bottom). Many of the zooplankton are no larger than the head of a pin, but this group of ocean drifters also includes shrimp and other crustaceans.

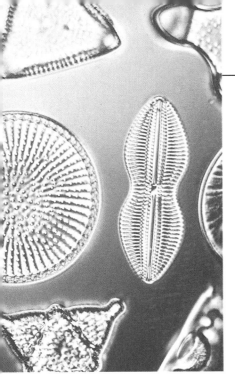

In turn, clams and other animals that filter dinoflagellates from the water accumulate the toxins, rendering their flesh poisonous to humans. The animals themselves are largely immune to the toxins. Illness and death from red-tide tainted shellfish have been reported since the time of the late-18th Century British explorer Captain George Vancouver, who lost at least one sailor to paralytic shellfish poisoning (PSP). Dinoflagellate toxin blocks nerve impulses, first causing a victim's lips, face and fingertips to tingle. Numbness, respiratory paralysis and death may follow. Medical science offers no antidote.

But the benefits far outweigh the occasional localized problems. Aside from their major role in oxygen and food production, phytoplankton absorb CO_2 dissolved in ocean water. This last function has taken on new importance recently as scientists have become concerned about the possibility of global warming caused by the greenhouse effect.

Sunlight reaches the Earth's atmosphere with a full palette of colors, or wavelengths. High-energy, short-wavelength light passes easily through the atmospheric window, striking the Earth and reradiating at a lower energy level. Some of this outgoing light is trapped by the atmosphere, which is opaque to longer-wavelength infrared; the rest escapes into space. With a buildup of carbon dioxide and several other gases in the atmosphere, however, more infrared is absorbed by the atmosphere and reradiated in all directions, heating the Earth's surface and causing the greenhouse effect. With more CO_2 in the atmosphere, scientists fear, the average temperature on earth could increase, perhaps as much as 6°F in the next half-century. Such an increase could lead to worldwide weather changes and widespread flooding as polar ice caps melt, raising the level of the oceans.

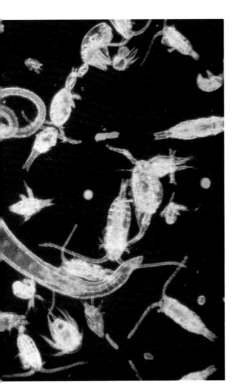

Of the CO_2 trapped by phytoplankton, some ends up in the tissue of the fishes that consume the organisms, but a fraction sinks, remaining in sediments for centuries. As much as 2.5 billion tons of carbon yearly are trapped in this manner. Phytoplankton may also counter the greenhouse effect in quite a different way. Some scientists theorize that a gas released by rapidly reproducing phytoplankton may increase the earth's cloud cover. The gas, called dimethylsulfide, works by providing nuclei, or kernels, around which water vapor can condense. The result is more clouds, which reflect more of the Sun's energy back into space, reducing temperatures on earth. Other scientists suggest artificially enhancing phytoplankton growth as an active method of reducing atmospheric CO_2 (*pages 134-135*).

A THREE-DIMENSIONAL REALM

In two dimensions, the oceans cover nearly three-quarters of the globe, one huge, interconnected mass of water. That medium is made even bigger because—unlike landbased animals—sea organisms live in three dimensions. Averaging more than 12,000 feet deep, the oceanic realm comprises some 300 million cubic miles, 250 times as much living space as on land.

In such a huge volume, food is diluted and mates are harder to find. But sea animals have developed ingenious ways to deal with these challenges. One species of sea slug secretes a mucus web many times as large as itself, then allows the web to sink slowly, skimming scarce plankton. When the net is full, the slug swallows it whole. Larvaceans, finger-sized, spineless relatives of the vertebrates, construct mucus houses to filter huge volumes of water and extract the food it contains;

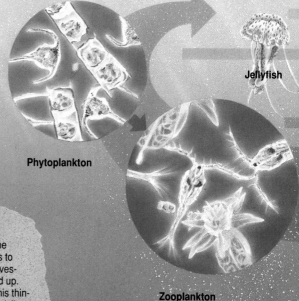

SUNLIT ZONE
Perhaps two-thirds of all the photosynthesis occuring on Earth takes place in this region. Extending down to 650 feet—beyond which light barely penetrates—the sunlit zone nourishes the plankton that form the base of the food web.

Jellyfish

Phytoplankton

Zooplankton

THE WEB OF LIFE

At a glance, the immensely diverse creatures that populate the oceanic realm seem too different to be related. In fact, they are all part of a web that ultimately links everything from microscopic algae to 100-ton whales in one gigantic cycle.

Ocean water, home to 250,000 known species, fills its basin like a layer cake in a pan. On top lies a rich, thin frosting, where plenty of light provides energy for the microscopic plants and algae—phytoplankton—to synthesize food. These "grasses of the sea" in turn feed a vast variety of drifting creatures called zooplankton. This cornucopia of plenty spirals up the food pyramid feeding a decreasing number of larger and larger fish. In a world of diminishing returns it takes 100 pounds of phytoplankton to produce just one pound of fish.

While most of the plankton and the free-swimming ocean denizens, known as the nekton, reside in the sunlit surface waters, some animal life is found at all levels, down to the deepest ocean floor. Below the level where light penetrates, fish and crustaceans are sustained by the organic debris that rains down from the food-rich surface waters.

Blowing winds sweep away warm surface water and draw up a continual rich supply of nutrients from a few hundred yards below the surface. Along with an infinitely slower upwelling from the ocean bottom, the replenishing from shallow water helps refuel the food chain and perpetuate the unending life cycle in the seas.

MESOPELAGIC ZONE
Beneath the sunlit level, the mesopelagic zone extends to 3,300 feet, where the last vestiges of light are swallowed up. Many of the creatures in this thinly populated zone migrate daily to the surface zone—rising at night to feed off the plankton that cluster there and then descending during the day to escape other predators.

BATHYPELAGIC ZONE
In this zone of utter darkness, with pressure of thousands of pounds per square inch, a strange collection of fish and squid eke out an existence. With food in short supply, animals have to be effective predators to take advantage of rare meals. Many have large mouths and very efficient teeth.

BENTHIC ZONE
Once it was thought that this zone was bereft of life. In fact, the ocean floor supports a surprising diversity of species made possible by the stability of the environment—the temperature hovers a few degrees above freezing—and the relatively constant supply of food that drifts down from the zones above.

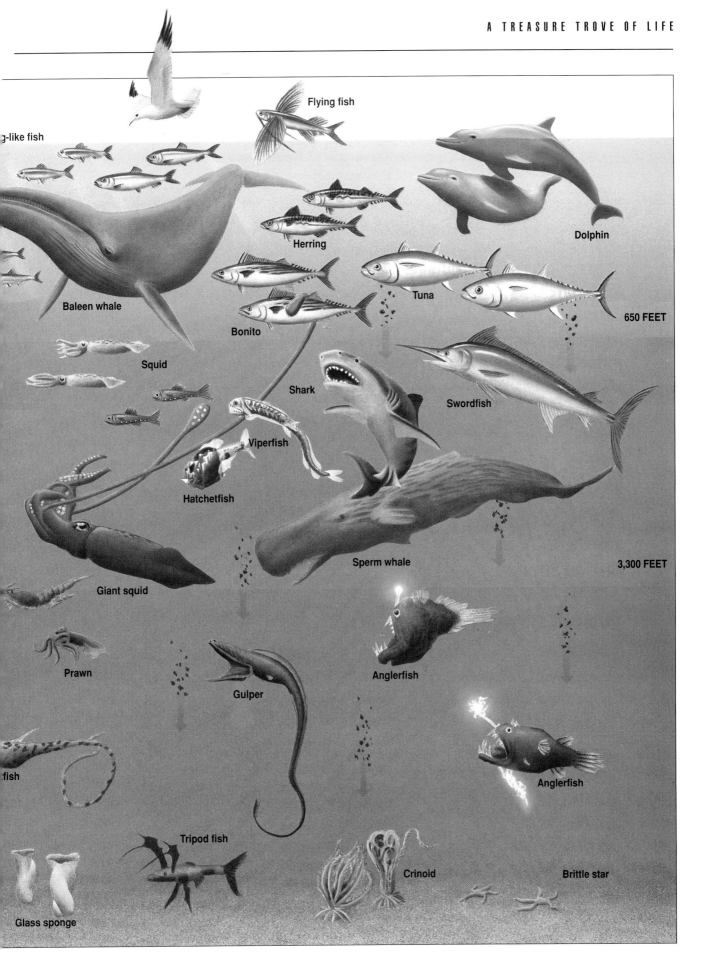

g-like fish

Flying fish

Baleen whale

Herring

Dolphin

Tuna

Bonito

650 FEET

Squid

Shark

Swordfish

Viperfish

Hatchetfish

Giant squid

Sperm whale

3,300 FEET

Prawn

Anglerfish

Gulper

Anglerfish

fish

Tripod fish

Crinoid

Brittle star

Glass sponge

55

some of these strange structures are as large as a person. In deep water, many fish make the most of any organism they meet, gulping down rare meals that may weigh as much as they do. Many sea animals cope with the paucity of mates by producing both sperm and eggs, so that any individual can mate with any other individual, regardless of its sex. Others change sex depending on their age or on the sex of their nearest neighbor. In some deep sea fishes, the males become parasites on females, always available to shed a few sperm.

Even phytoplankton, which make their own food, must make the most of what little is at hand. Like plants in a garden, phytoplankton need fertilizer such as nitrates and phosphates. Rich garden soil contains about one-half of one percent nitrate, 10,000 times more than the richest seawater. Furthermore, wastes and carcasses sink at sea, removing fertilizer from the surface.

Those nutrients eventually descend to the ocean floor where they supply an entire community with the sustenance it needs to survive. On their slow drift to the bottom of the ocean, the nutrients pass through a zone of twilight, underneath the sunlit zone, extending from 650 to 3,300 feet. Known as the mesopelagic zone, this region is characterized by a vertical migration of life that moves upward during the night and downward during the day. During daylight hours, zooplankton descend from the surface layer to the darker regions below to avoid detection. At night, they rise back towards the surface. As the plankton shift up and down so do the predators who feed on them and the predators who feed on the predators, in a majestic migration that measures its pulse by the Sun.

One of the phenomena created by this migration came to be called the deep scattering layer during World War II. While testing sonar—a device that bounces sound rays off an object to determine its distance—U.S. Navy researchers discovered reflections from much shallower depths than expected. Tracked day and night, this "bottom" rose and fell. Its source was unknown, but its military importance as a possible camouflage for submarines was obvious. The discovery was classified as a military secret; later, the planktonic nature of the layer was recognized.

A WORLD OF FISH

Three large groups of fish inhabit the ocean. The most primitive, called jawless fish, include the scavenging hagfishes and parasitic lampreys. More refined are the fish with skeletons of cartilage rather than bone, the rays and the sharks, which most certainly have jaws. But the most evolutionarily advanced and most wildly varied fish are those with bony skeletons.

Among the many adaptations of fish to a pelagic life, two stand out. In a three-dimensional environment with little light, fish have developed a sensory system unknown on land. This lateral line system consists of gelatin-filled canals under the skin which open through pores to the water. Like the inner ear of terrestrial vertebrates, these canals are lined with sensory hairs that send signals to the brain when they are bent. Any change in water movement—such as that caused by a meal or an enemy swimming nearby—jiggles the gelatin and wiggles the hairs. Along with their eyes, which in some species are 100 times more sensitive than our own, fish use this system to sense precise three-dimensional position.

To maintain their position in the water, bony fish have evolved a unique flotation system to compensate for their weight. Called the swim bladder, it evolved from lungs left behind as early fish became ever more committed to a watery habitat. The gas-filled sac acts as an internal float, counteracting the weight of bone and muscle. Blood vessels surrounding the swim bladder precisely adjust inflation by secreting or absorbing oxygen, making bony fish the masters of their medium, able to escape or attack by moving forward, backward, vertically or horizontally with equal ease. At great depth, however, gas becomes an impractical float material—it is too compressible—so deep-sea fish have developed bladders filled with light, noncompressible oil.

Fish have put their ability to move precisely to good use in a behavior called schooling. Gathering in groups that can range from a leaderless trio to a 17-mile-long, million-member run of herring, fish in schools often behave like a single, gigantic individual. Though their arrangement in space remains neither constant nor geometric, they can turn as one, more smoothly than a marching band. Feeding, mating and escaping all come easier in schools.

Coordination in a school shifts from precise to spectacular when a predator pursues or attacks. A hungry barracuda deciding exactly which fish to eat—no mean feat when faced with a constantly changing, flickering mob of thousands—may suddenly find itself ahead of the school rather than behind it.

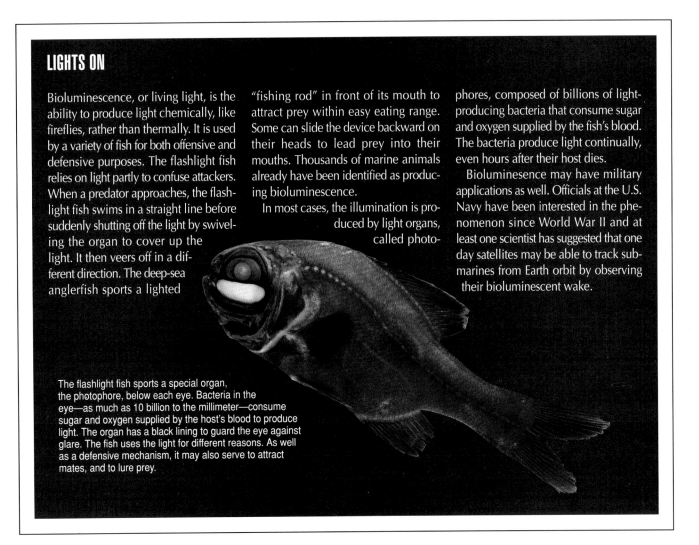

LIGHTS ON

Bioluminescence, or living light, is the ability to produce light chemically, like fireflies, rather than thermally. It is used by a variety of fish for both offensive and defensive purposes. The flashlight fish relies on light partly to confuse attackers. When a predator approaches, the flashlight fish swims in a straight line before suddenly shutting off the light by swiveling the organ to cover up the light. It then veers off in a different direction. The deep-sea anglerfish sports a lighted "fishing rod" in front of its mouth to attract prey within easy eating range. Some can slide the device backward on their heads to lead prey into their mouths. Thousands of marine animals already have been identified as producing bioluminescence.

In most cases, the illumination is produced by light organs, called photophores, composed of billions of light-producing bacteria that consume sugar and oxygen supplied by the fish's blood. The bacteria produce light continually, even hours after their host dies.

Bioluminesence may have military applications as well. Officials at the U.S. Navy have been interested in the phenomenon since World War II and at least one scientist has suggested that one day satellites may be able to track submarines from Earth orbit by observing their bioluminescent wake.

The flashlight fish sports a special organ, the photophore, below each eye. Bacteria in the eye—as much as 10 billion to the millimeter—consume sugar and oxygen supplied by the host's blood to produce light. The organ has a black lining to guard the eye against glare. The fish uses the light for different reasons. As well as a defensive mechanism, it may also serve to attract mates, and to lure prey.

King of the Ocean

Long before dinosaurs first roamed the planet, even before the time when insects first flew, sharks glided gracefully through the world's oceans. With more than 300 million years of history behind them, sharks have evolved into a marvelously sophisticated organism, fit to live at the pinnacle of the ocean's animal kingdom.

The forward part of the shark's body is flattened to reduce drag during rapid turning and to allow sideways movement during normal swimming. The bulging middle section acts as a fulcrum when the shark turns, allowing it to pivot quickly. A vertical fin on the back and two pectoral fins projecting downward from the sides serve a variety of functions, from providing lift and aiding acceleration to assisting in braking and turning. The long caudal fin or tail—the upper lobe is always longer than the lower—provides the thrust, propelling some sharks at more than 40 miles an hour during sprints.

Unlike other fish, sharks have no gas bladders to change their buoyancy. Instead, their large, oily livers give them this ability. Up to 20 percent of a blue shark's weight can be made up by its liver. Different species also have different densities depending on where they live. Active swimmers such as pelagic sharks, which spend their lives near the surface, are more dense and therefore less neutrally buoyant than their languid, bottom-dwelling counterparts. Sharks near the ocean floor expend less energy to maintain their position.

The shark's sense of smell is legendary. Scientific studies show that the creature can detect blood diluted to a ratio of 1 part in 100 million. That ability is made possible by nasal sacs—folded tissue inside the nostrils. A flap across the opening causes water to flow in one side and out the other, generating a continual supply of water for smelling.

The shark's flexibility is enhanced by the fact that cartilage and connective tissue—more flexible and lighter than bone—provide the framework for its body.

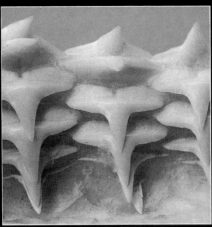

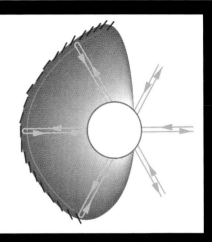

The shark's skin consists of dermal prominences—actually modified teeth—which
give the skin a rough, sandpaper-like texture. But instead of increasing drag and
slowing down the shark, these denticles
channel the water, resulting in a flow that
acts to reduce friction.

Because of their powerful bites and the
tearing action of their method of eating,
sharks frequently lose teeth. New scalpel-
sharp teeth form in a groove on the inside
of the jaw and move forward on a membrane called a tooth bed, continually
replacing the broken or blunted ones.

A shark's eye features a series of reflecting
plates at the back of the eye, behind the
retina, known as tapetal plates. These function like mirrors, reflecting up to 90 percent
of certain colors of light back into the light-
receptor cells of the eye, enhancing the
shark's ability to see.

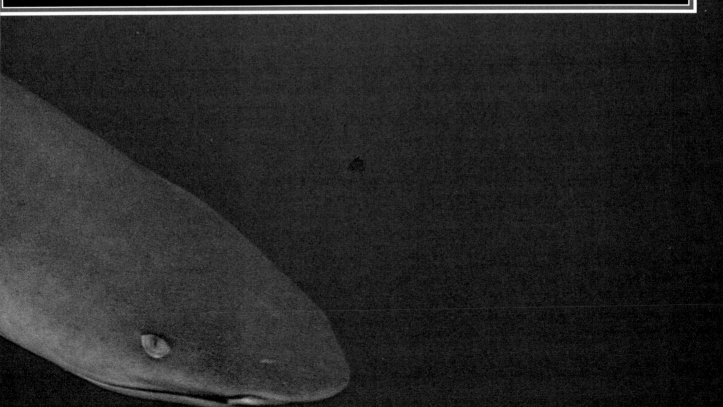

Almost as if responding to a precise command, half of the school swings left and half right, re-forming behind the pursuer in a maneuver dubbed the fountain effect. If the barracuda mounts another attack, the tactic is repeated.

Under flank attack, a school may suddenly explode, like the big shell in a fireworks finale. In the blink of an eye, each fish accelerates from a standstill to a velocity of up to 20 body lengths per second. No mere every-fish-for-itself rout, each individual darts away from the attacker on a radius. Somehow each fish "knows" where its neighbor will go. The entire expansion can occur in less than a second. Fish rely on visual cues as well as lateral line information to stay in formation; where information from the two sources contradict each other, the latter takes precedence. Scientists studying schooling have never observed collisions unless the errant fish has lost at least one of the two senses.

CREATURES OF THE DEEP

While the concentration of fish—and indeed all life in the oceans—is highest in the sunlit and mesopelagic zones, the world below hardly is bereft of life. Beneath the mesopelagic zone, where twilight dwindles to a solid, disorienting darkness, lies the bathypelagic—or deep pelagic—zone. Animals are scarce, but as this inhospitable realm comprises nearly 80 percent of the Earth's habitable volume, abyssal animals make up a huge biomass. The tiny bristle-jawed fish, for example, are perhaps the most numerous fish in the world. Since there is no light, scarce organisms of the abyss rely not on photosynthesis, but on the organic particles that drift down from above.

The abyssal fish are a bizarre-looking collection of minuscule monstrosities, with names like black swallower, dragonfish and fangtooth. Besides mouths to match their monikers, deep-sea fishes sport other odd adaptations to darkness. Some lack eyes altogether. Others stare with huge orbs tuned precisely to the few blue light waves that penetrate to 1,600 feet. Still others have evolved tubular, upward-pointing eyes, ideal for seeing silhouettes of prey against the dim glow from above. Although most fish in this zone are usually weak-bodied and generally are not more than six inches long, they still manage to appear fearsome, with greatly extendible jaws and expandable abdomens so that they can take advantage of the rare meal that may pass by.

At the lowest level of the open ocean lies an environment at once strange and strangely familiar. This benthic, or bottom, environment resembles a desert, with little life. Organisms living here must not only survive without producers—the plankton and bacteria that form the base of the food chain—they must survive where water pressure may reach several tons per square inch. Yet the bottom is two-dimensional like the land humans live on. Organic material remains in a layer on the surface. And the bottom, like land, varies from place to place. It may be rocky or smooth, steep or flat, hard or soft. Though 88 percent of all marine species live on the bottom, nearly all occur near shore. Among the cast of characters attached to the bottom of the deep sea are the simplest animals, the sponges, and some of the most ancient, the sea lilies, both of which wait for currents to waft detritus onto their feeding structures. A few such creatures in several square meters was once thought to represent a dense bottom fauna. That was until Corliss' and Edmond's 1977 expedition to the ocean floor.

LIFE WITHOUT LIGHT

First discovered near the Galápagos Islands in 1977, the community of life surrounding hot vents of water gushing up from the ocean floor astounded marine biologists. Here, thousands of feet below the surface of the ocean, were creatures that derived their sustenance not from light, which drives photosynthesis, but from a chemical synthesis based on hydrogen sulfide (H_2S).

The source of the H_2S is water that seeps through the ocean floor and comes in contact with underlying hot rock, which heats the water and produces hydrogen sulfide. The water is then expelled through the ocean floor and feeds bacteria that live in some of the organisms surrounding the vents. In a symbiotic relationship, the bacteria use the hydrogen sulfide to produce food in return for protection offered by their host organisms.

As well as proving that life can produce food without light, the hydrothermal vents have caused some scientists to speculate that life on Earth may have begun in similar communities several billion years ago. While the Earth's surface was bombarded by ultraviolet rays—before the ozone layer wrapped a protective blanket around the planet—hydrothermal vents of the ocean floor may have offered a safe habitat to nurture life in its earliest forms.

1. In areas where two of the rigid plates that form the outer shell—or lithosphere—of the Earth pull apart, a viscous molten material called magma rises from the planet's interior to fill the gap. Cold, dense water that seeps through cracks in the sea floor comes into contact with the superheated rock above the magma. The water is heated and becomes saturated with a number of minerals. It is also chemically altered: Oxygen atoms are stripped off sulphate ions, which are common in seawater, and gain hydrogen to become hydrogen sulphide.

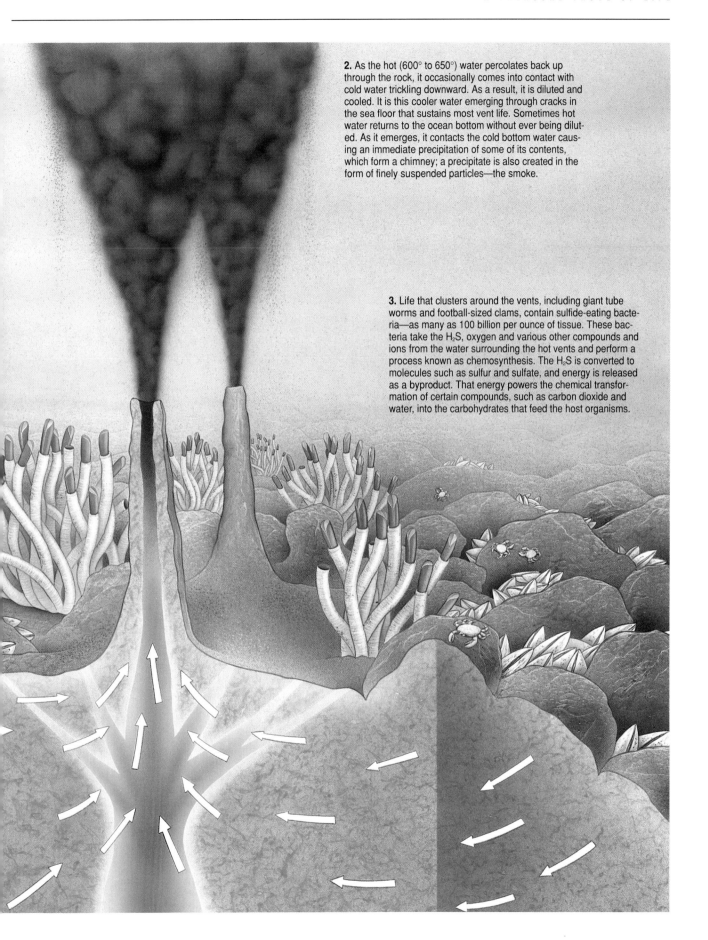

2. As the hot (600° to 650°) water percolates back up through the rock, it occasionally comes into contact with cold water trickling downward. As a result, it is diluted and cooled. It is this cooler water emerging through cracks in the sea floor that sustains most vent life. Sometimes hot water returns to the ocean bottom without ever being diluted. As it emerges, it contacts the cold bottom water causing an immediate precipitation of some of its contents, which form a chimney; a precipitate is also created in the form of finely suspended particles—the smoke.

3. Life that clusters around the vents, including giant tube worms and football-sized clams, contain sulfide-eating bacteria—as many as 100 billion per ounce of tissue. These bacteria take the H_2S, oxygen and various other compounds and ions from the water surrounding the hot vents and perform a process known as chemosynthesis. The H_2S is converted to molecules such as sulfur and sulfate, and energy is released as a byproduct. That energy powers the chemical transformation of certain compounds, such as carbon dioxide and water, into the carbohydrates that feed the host organisms.

One of the most peculiar creatures to be found around the hydrothermal vents is Riftia pachyptila—a six-foot-long tube worm topped by a red feathery plume composed of 200,000 tiny tentacles. With no gut, no mouth and no anus, the worm is incapable of capturing its own food. Instead, it is fed by the bacteria that live in an organ called a trophosome, which occupies most of the tube worm's body.

The huge clams that cluster around the vents are nourished by symbiotic bacteria. The bacteria play a role as central to the hot-vent communities as phytoplankton do in the main ocean food web.

NIGHT LIFE

When a group of oceanographers set out to explore a subterranean mountain range near the Galápagos Islands off Ecuador, no one expected to discover an unknown community of creatures, and it took some time before researchers understood how the ecosystem—and others discovered later in the Atlantic Ocean—flourished. After all, the basis of life, most scientists believed, was the Sun, which produces the necessary carbohydrates to sustain life. But there is no light on the deep ocean floor, and yet somehow creatures like giant, crimson-tipped worms and dinner-plate-sized clams survive there, deriving their sustenance not from the gentle rain of detritus from the sunlit regions of the ocean far above, but from some other source. Scientists puzzled over what that source could be.

The answer turned out to be a chemical form of synthesis based on hydrogen sulfide (H_2S). The creatures that surround hot springs on the ocean floor, like the six-foot-long tube worms (called *Riftia pachyptila*—thick feathers of the rift) contain bacteria that use hydrogen sulfide and oxygen (O_2) extracted from the water to produce energy. That energy serves, in essence, as a substitute for sunlight. It allows the bacteria to convert carbon dioxide and water to carbohydrates. The result of this chemosynthesis is the same as photosynthesis: the production of ingredients necessary to sustain life. Only the source of the energy is different.

The tube worm bacteria are symbiotic, supplying food for its host in return for a continual supply of the raw ingredients for chemosynthesis and a safe haven to carry on their activity. Supplying the bacteria with oxygen and carbon dioxide comes easily; a bright red plume that crowns the creature functions like a fish's gill, absorbing carbon dioxide and oxygen from the sea water and releasing carbon dioxide. Just as in humans, veins filled with rich, red blood transport oxygen.

Supplying H_2S to the bacteria is another matter. Hydrogen sulfide poisons most organisms with a chemical action and a toxicity similar to cyanide. By chemically binding to hemoglobin—the substance in red blood cells that transports oxygen—in place of the oxygen, H_2S asphyxiates organisms. But the tube worms not only survive in water rich in H_2S, they actively absorb the chemical from sea water and transport it in their blood. An evolutionary change in the hemoglobin of the tube worms solves the poisoning problem neatly. *Riftia* hemoglobin contains separate binding sites for both O_2 and H_2S. This mechanism protects the worm from the toxic effects of H_2S and also ensures safe delivery of the energy-rich molecule to the bacteria.

Marine biologists suspect that other symbiotic pairs in the vent community evolved independently, because the bacterial strains living in each species are not identical. Vent clams deal with potential H_2S poisoning differently from the tube worms. The clams evolved a special protein that binds H_2S to the bacteria living in the clam's gills. With a plentiful supply of food, these clams filter food from the water only weakly, if at all, they have relatively high metabolic rates and grow fast—one and a half inches per year—reaching a full foot in length at maturity. In the normal deep sea, bivalaves are small, probably because of the scarcity of food. The way large, yellow vent mussels deal with H_2S remains unknown.

Other vent organisms rely on bacteria only indirectly, but still have to cope with poisonous H_2S in the water. White crabs probably act as scavengers or predators. They dispose of H_2S in their food by chemically converting it in a liver-like organ.

Vent communities in the Atlantic have provided other surprises to scientists. The lack of eyes on a two-inch shrimp collected in this lightless environment caused no surprise among marine biologists. But while examining the shrimp in the lab, scientist Cindy Van Dover found large pigmented patches on its back. Further research led to the startling conclusion that the patches function as eyes. Van Dover believes the shrimp detect the faint glow of super hot water, perhaps to avoid being cooked. (A heat-sensing organ would perform a similar function, but visual organs respond to stimuli more quickly.) Others suggest the shrimp detect bioluminescence that human eyes and electronic sensors have not yet seen. That light would signal light-producing creatures that, for the shrimp, could be food.

Deep-sea communities also have been found surrounding cold seeps of crude petroleum and natural gas, or methane. In both cases, bacteria appear to garner energy by breaking down either H_2S or methane. Mussels from methane seeps can survive in labs even if natural gas is bubbled through their aquarium water.

BETWEEN LAND AND SEA

Biological activity in the deep-vent communities is highly productive—1,000 times greater than the rest of the deep-ocean floor—but still pales in diversity compared with life near the surface regions. Nowhere is that more pronounced than at the interface between land and sea. Here, an intricate web of creatures must survive the daily pulse of tides, buffeted by winds and lashed by waves. Many kinds of bottom exist between the highest and lowest tides: mud flats, sandy surfing beaches, near-vertical cliffs. But biologically, the richest of these environments is the rocky intertidal community.

An observer walking toward the water during a very low tide quickly sees several distinguishing features of this community that straddles two realms. First, many attached organisms lie exposed to the air. Second, the mixture of organisms changes, sometimes abruptly. On rocky shores with a tide rise of more than six feet, these changes are reflected in different zones or bands, each populated by a particular well-adapted collection of plants and animals.

At the uppermost reaches of the rocky intertidal community lies a band moistened only occasionally by waves, called the splash zone, which forms a transition area between the land and the sea. Black marine lichens may mark the upper edge of this zone. These common crusty or leafy-looking organisms represent yet another symbiosis, a mat of fungus fibers surrounding numerous cells of green algae. Lichens thrive in harsh rocky environments on land, but are not truly marine organisms. Cyanobacteria, whose protective slime saves them from dehydration, coat the splash-zone rocks. Several kinds of terrestrial insects flit from rock to rock, but the only truly marine animals are the bright green isopods—small crustaceans—and small black snails. Both stand with one foot on land and the other in the sea. They migrate up and down between the splash zone and the highest entirely marine environment, the upper intertidal zone. Here the splash zone's flat-black band of lichens and cyanobacteria often changes abruptly to a rough white stripe, the realm of the acorn barnacle.

The sturdy, limestone shell of a barnacle, permanently cemented to the rock, may mislead the casual observer as it misled early biologists. Although it may closely resemble the clam, the barnacle is not a mollusk. It has antennae and joint-

LIFE ON THE ROCKS

On rocky coasts where oceans touch land, a dense and diverse community of land-adapted marine life dwells. The community's still-life appearance seems to defy the hostile conditions that torment it: waves, winds, tides and temperatures—not to mention competition for food and space.

Distinguishable by a band of color that horizontally stripes the rock, each zone is home to a cast of characters shaped by the conditions reigning there. The highest perch, the splash zone, is sparsely inhabited by a few creatures that have adapted to an arid existence on land. The spray from a breaking wave or rain is their only relief from constant exposure to the salty air and Sun.

Beneath the splash zone, the high intertidal residents take advantage of the ocean's brief visit at high tide for food and water. They store enough supplies to endure long hours when the tide is out.

The middle intertidal zone creatures are attuned to the rhythm of the tides that submerge and expose them twice daily. They also have evolved the art of clinging tenaciously, resisting the constant pounding of breaking waves.

A sanctuary of sorts is found in the low intertidal zone. Here, a security-blanket of water wards off exterior dangers and offers an abundance of food for its many species. However, a booming population makes food and space something to fight for. Moreover, this zone is a feeding ground for hungry predators that venture up from the deep.

Lichen
Microscopic algae lie within slimy cases of fungus that protect them against air and Sun's dehydrating powers. Lichen carpet the splash zone in patches.

Rough Periwinkle
Creeps between the splash and the high intertidal zone, feeding on microscopic algae. It has a rough surfaced tongue to rasp algae from rock.

Whelk
Roams both the high and middle intertidal zones. It mounts its victim, softens the victim's shell with a mucus secretion, bores a hole through the shell and sucks out the soft innards.

Barnacle
Feeds at high tide by straining plankton with rake-like feet protruding from its shell. At low tide it withdraws its feet and seals the opening with a door-like membrane, storing water and food.

Rock Crab
Rises to the shore during spring and summer. It feeds off detritus (the remains of plants and animals) and occasionally feasts on a live worm or shrimp.

Mussel
Secures itself to rock at the middle intertidal level with black threads called byssus, secreted by its foot. It then opens its shell and filters microscopic organisms from water.

SPLASH ZONE
Creatures who live in the uppermost of the four zones of the rocky intertidal shore must survive only on spray from breakers and rainfall. It is the most barren of the four strata.

HIGH INTERTIDAL ZONE
Extending down to the average high-tide marks, the second-highest zone is washed by tidewater only several hours a month. Barnacles are its most visible tenants.

MIDDLE INTERTIDAL ZONE
Subjected to tides twice daily, this area is the one intertidal zone completely covered and uncovered by water every day. The middle intertidal boasts a crowded community, shaped not only by a wave-battered environment but also by strong interaction and competition between its residents.

LOW INTERTIDAL ZONE
Covered by water almost continually, this zone is populated mostly by creatures of the sea, able to endure only the briefest and rarest exposure to air. This zone is bared only a few hours each month by exceptionally low tides.

Red Algae
Exposed only during neap tides. The purple-red leaves absorb minerals from the water and trap energy from the Sun—essential for photosynthesis.

Bladderwrack
Clings to the middle intertidal zone and the top of the lower intertidal, using splayed frond fingers called holdfasts. Liquid-filled bladders provide buoyancy in water.

Starfish
Clings to low intertidal zone rocks, or moves along them, using the suction power of minuscule, tube-like feet. The feet are also used to hold prey and to pull in the meal.

Kelp
The leathery fronds dominate the low intertidal zone. Undulating beneath the waves, the kelp extracts minerals, concentrating them into the liquid of their cells.

Sea Anemone
Compensating for immobility, the anemone uses its tentacles to launch paralyzing darts into small animals that pass within reach.

Sea Urchin
Sports spiny quills attached by ball-and-socket joints, which allow omnidirectional movement. The urchin uses its spines to defend itself against predators.

65

ed legs and is actually a crustacean cousin of the crab—a fact only discovered in 1830 when marine biologists first found barnacle larvae. When a larva washes up on a rock with a little space available, it permanently attaches head down and metamorphoses into an adult, secreting six fused shell plates. The volcano-shaped shell, which withstands waves smashing the beach at up to 6,000 pounds per square foot, can be hermetically sealed with a four-part door during low tides. When the water rises, the barnacle rakes the water with its feathery legs, filtering out morsels of detritus and plankton.

Between barnacle patches, other animals graze the rock surfaces. Limpets—conical-shelled, big-footed relatives of snails—slide slowly over the rocks, scraping the thin slime of algae with a rough tonguelike organ. Small snails, shore crabs, and hermit crabs also frequent this zone.

Most intertidal producers, phytoplankton and algae, live no higher than the upper intertidal, where at least some water is available. Diatoms create a microscopic lawn on any bare rock surfaces. Algae called rockweeds may cover rocks big enough not to be rolled around in the surf. Rockweed survives wave action because of sturdy stems and strong attachments, called holdfasts. Small jelly-filled floats hold them upright when the tide comes in.

In the middle intertidal zone, the area between the average high tide and the average low tide, live animals and algae that depend on the twice daily drenching to stay alive. As the acorn barnacle defines the upper intertidal, the blue mussel defines this zone. Anyone who has ever tried to pull a mussel from a rock can attest to its fitness for living on a wave-battered coast. The mussel's almost aerodynamic shape, combined with its strong anchors, called byssus threads, allow it to withstand relentless pounding. Not only are the byssus threads themselves strong, but the mussel glues the threads to rocks underwater with an adhesive unmatched by any synthetic adhesive devised by humans. Only recently identified by scientists, it has proved difficult to synthesize. Still, efforts persist; many feel that the glue's ability to harden and hold under wet and chemically tough conditions may have a variety of applications, from bone repair and eye surgery to repairing ships without dry-docking.

On, under and between the rocks of the middle intertidal zone live a profusion of animals of nearly every phylum known to science. Mollusks are represented by small and large snails, the eight-plated chitons, wildly colorful sea slugs, and even the occasional small octopus hiding in a tidal pool. Myriad shore crabs, kelp crabs, hermit crabs, shrimps and isopods—small crustaceans—fill the roster of arthropods, the animals with jointed legs. The radially symmetrical echinoderms are here too, sea stars in orange, vermilion and purple; sea urchins with purple, green or crimson spines; and slug-shaped sea cucumbers ranging in color from conservative white to blazing orange. Members of small phyla—unnoticed by most beachcombers—abound, including flatworms, ribbon worms, roundworms and marine relatives of the earthworm. Even the phylum to which humans belong—the chordates—holds its own, not only with tiny tide pool fish, but with attached relatives of the pelagic larvaceans, called sea squirts.

The density of animals and algae explodes in the lowest of the four zones—the lower intertidal. Here, animals like starfish and urchins bathe in food 24 hours a day, every day of the year. Large fast-growing algae called kelp dominate the lower intertidal, providing food not only for animals grazing directly on the blades, but for many others as well. Kelp blades grow like hair, sloughing off at the tips, and the bits of kelp tissue add clouds of nutrients to the water.

LIFE IN THE CORAL REEFS

At the base of the rocky shores off the U.S. West Coast—the richest intertidal habitat in temperate climes—forests of kelp and tons of phytoplankton turn the water green, and support many species of fish and invertebrates. In tropical waters, on the other hand, almost no phytoplankton color the water, and yet coral reefs in these warm, crystal blue waters may be the richest environment on Earth. Tropical coral reefs' ecosystems compare in their colorful complexity and lush productivity to tropical rain forests. But that very richness poses a problem similar to that of the hydrothermal vent communities. In these nutrient-poor waters, where are the producers who feed the consumers?

The problem did not occur to early scientists. Until 1723, most naturalists thought the twig-like corals were plants. In that year, a French naturalist, Jean André Peyssonel, described corals in detail, concluding that the branching forms were colonial animals, not plants. His view was derided and the thesis was rejected by the French Academy of Sciences. Peyssonel spent the rest of his life as a scientist-in-exile in the Caribbean. When London's Royal Society finally published the work—30 years after its initial rejection—Peyssonel's name was suppressed.

But Peyssonel's observations eventually prevailed. Related to jellyfish and sea anemones, the large, branching structure now called a coral actually consists of an interconnected colony of individuals named polyps, typically a fraction of an inch in diameter. Each polyp resembles a tiny anemone, with a cup-shaped body opening through a mouth ringed with tentacles. Bridges of tissue connect adjacent polyps, allowing them to share food and react to stimuli in a coordinated fashion. These tiny, gelatinous animals, without brain or backbone, build structures surpassing any made by humans. A single reef may outweigh all human construction put together. But corals are slow builders. Australia's Great Barrier Reef first began to develop about 25 million years ago.

Every coral colony begins as a planktonic larva, nearly identical to those of a sea anemone and a jellyfish. Billions of the larvae course the ocean every second. Some settle and form colonies with flexible skeletons. Like the barnacle of the intertidal, a reef-building hard coral larva settles permanently, usually on another coral skeleton. The young polyp extracts calcium and carbonate from sea water, depositing these compounds in a cup-shaped, limestone shell around its body, its soft tissue overflowing the stoneware cup.

A coral polyp then proceeds to reproduce asexually, new polyps budding from the edge of the parent. In time a colony—a clone of polyps—forms, each polyp welding its skeleton to the growing colony. A single mature colony—as large as a living room—may weigh several hundred tons and contain billions of polyps. Hard coral colonies grow in a variety of shapes—tree-like, solid hemispheres with a surface pattern like a brain, or towers so tall they may be toppled by a hurricane.

These limy shapes form reefs thousands of feet thick in a process suggested by Charles Darwin in 1842. Corals, Darwin theorized, must begin building a fringing reef near the shores of a new volcanic island. As the volcano and the rift upon which it rests cool over the millennia, they sink, forcing colonies to grow upward to remain near the surface. Soon the volcano becomes a small island with a ring called a barrier reef surrounding it. Later the volcano may disappear altogether, leaving only parts of the ring, called an atoll. A century after Darwin's observations, when geologists drilled cores 4,200 feet into Eniwetok Atoll between Hawaii and Borneo, they found the volcanic rock Darwin had predicted.

The organisms filling every chink and covering every surface affect the physical infrastructure of the reef as well as the biological community. Coral animals manufacture a framework. Certain algae, featuring a hard, limy exoskeleton, contribute tons of limestone sand to fill in the spaces, and a "cement," probably produced by bacteria, binds the stony whole together. Sponges, sea worms and mollusks chip away the surface or bore holes, sometimes fatally weakening the structure.

To gain energy to produce such structures, coral polyps eat much like sea anemones. Waiting at night with outstretched tentacles, they gorge on detritus or plankton. Nematocysts, tiny stinging cells in their tentacles, paralyze prey with miniature harpoons. Yet despite feeding all night, corals derive less than 15 percent of their nutrition from plankton. Not until the 1950s did marine biologists understand how corals get enough to eat. In the process they discovered the missing producers in the coral reef community.

Not unlike hydrothermal vent tube worms, corals depend on a symbiotic relationship to flourish. But instead of chemosynthetic bacteria, coral cells contain single-celled algae. Exposed to sunlight during the day, while the polyp stays retracted, the algae benefit from optimum CO_2 and dissolved nutrients—the polyp's wastes. At night, while the polyp feeds, the algae—known as zooxanthellae—leak sugars, starches and other nutrients into the cells of the polyp. The prodigious productivity of the coral reef ecosystem depends on this symbiosis. The fact that producers exist inside benthic organisms rooted to the ocean floor also explains the distribution of coral reefs. Because they rely on sunlight penetration, these animals only grow in clear, relatively shallow tropical seas.

A reef community may include more species than any other ecosystem. Hundreds of corals and algae, and thousands of species of fish and mollusks may live in one reef system. The corals themselves play multiple parts, functioning as producers and consumers. Among this variety biologists have found a surprising number of symbioses in addition to the corals and their resident algae, and in each case the relationship works a little differently.

Sea anemones participate in several symbioses. Anemones fall prey to certain predators despite their formidable protection. Some sea slugs nip the tips of anemone tentacles, stinging cells and all. But while the slug digests the soft tissue, the nematocysts remain unharmed, passing through the slug's body to the fingerlike projections that cover its back. There, the nematocysts remain, providing defense for the slug that ate them.

The clownfish—named for its herky-jerky swimming style as well as its orange and white stripes—uses the anemone's stinging cells in a different way. Nematocysts fire only in response to a touch paired with a taste. By gingerly sideswiping the anemone, the fish gradually accumulates a layer of the anemone's own mucus, rendering the fish chemically invisible. If a diver experimentally removes the fish's mucus it quickly becomes an anemone meal. Twenty-six species of clownfish form

Australia's Great Barrier Reef stretches for 1,200 miles along the continent's east coast and is the greatest structure built by any living thing—man included. Created by colonies of coral polyps, simple creatures that secrete a calcareous shell, coral reefs support one of the richest and most diverse collections of life on the planet.

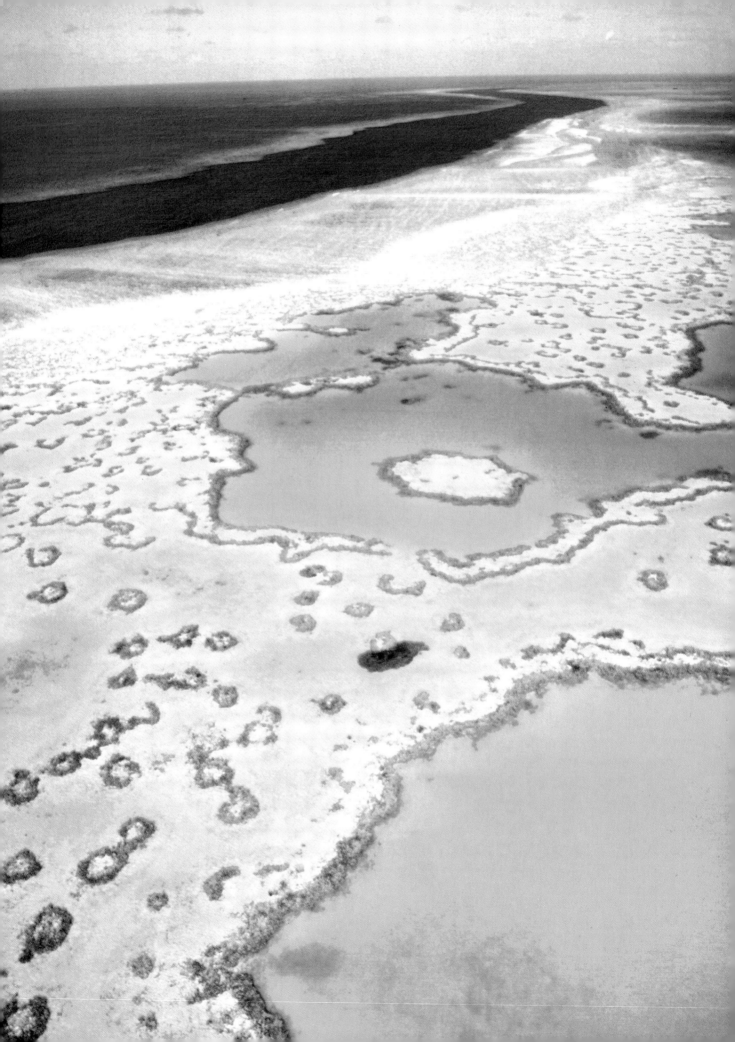

symbioses, eating leftovers from anemone meals and deriving staunch protection from their hosts. Clownfish may drop bits of food into the anemone, draw prey into the tentacles, eat parasites or chase anemone nibblers.

Not every relationship in a community benefits both parties. Predators and prey coevolve over millennia, each advance matched by a counteradvance. Sea urchins with six-inch poison-tipped spines live among the corals of the Red Sea. While some small fish hide among the spines—much as clownfish hide among anemone tentacles—no fish can risk a frontal attack to eat the urchin. The trigger fish, however, has developed a safe strategy. With a huff and a puff, it blows a jet of water, rolling the urchin over like a tumbleweed and exposing its vulnerable underside. Urchins, in their turn, enhance their spiny protection by hiding in coral crevices during the day and grazing only at night, while the trigger fish sleeps.

For organisms living among the coral, hiding comes easily. But in open sand flats, animals must make their own hideaways. Fields of pipe eels waft upright in the current, feeding on plankton, and apparently easy prey for any passing predator. At the slightest disturbance, every eel pops into the sand, tail first.

Nearly every living thing becomes fair game for another living thing, and the corals are no exception. Constantly nipping at corals, parrotfish eat not just the soft parts, but the stony skeletons as well, passing tons of sand every year. As they scrape away living tissue, parrotfish provide fresh areas for algae and planktonic larvae to settle. The resulting algal lawn may cover 80 percent of a reef's surface,

Master builder of the coral reef, the coral polyp (below) feeds through a digestive cavity, nourishing one-celled algae called zooxanthellae that live inside it. In return, the microscopic plants promote the polyp's secretion of limestone, which forms the coral reef's permanent structure. Such symbiotic relationships are widespread throughout the coral reef community. Witness also the clownfish and the sea anemone (right). Swimming unharmed among the poisoned tentacles of the sea anemone, the colorful clownfish lures unsuspecting prey into its host's deadly barbs. In exchange for attracting food to the anemone, the clownfish receives protection from its own enemies.

feeding myriad grazing animals. Another coral scraper, an herbivore called the threespot damselfish, nips living coral, then "farms" the resulting algal crop.

Having survived predators, hurricanes and even atomic explosions, a reef may succumb to overly warm water, possibly caused by global warming. When they are too warm, corals expel their symbiotic algae, turning from green to white. This bleaching causes reproduction to stop, and may kill whole colonies. First noted in 1987, widespread bleaching occurred again in 1989 and 1990. If global warming is at fault—and scientists are not agreed—coral bleaching could accelerate, as corals remove significant amounts of CO_2 from the atmosphere.

The maze of cracks and crevices created by corals rooted to the ocean floor provides homes for the innumerable life forms of coral reefs. But not all the sea's organisms need to be attached. In the southwest Atlantic lies another shallow-water community, based not on corals or seashore rocks, but on floating seaweed.

ADRIFT IN THE SARGASSO SEA

On September 16, 1492, Columbus sailed into a part of the Atlantic with weather "like April in Andalusia" and in this benign climate, his little fleet was soon surrounded by rafts of floating seaweeds. So close lay the weed that Columbus' men feared it might trap them forever. But the vessels sailed safely on, and Columbus, describing the weed and its pea-sized floats in his journal, surmised that it had originally come from coastal rocks. Millions of tons of the seaweed

Masters of Disguise

In a world based on survival of the fittest, the secret to success is learning how to avoid becoming a neighbor's dinner. The technique involved may be simply seeking safety in numbers and traveling in a school; or it might be a well-timed extra flick of the tail. Or it could be a disguise so devilishly deceptive that other fish fail to see it—or see it and believe it is something else.

Fish are some of the world's most artful camouflagers, capable of fooling predators and scientists alike. (It is not uncommon to find museum collections with a fish and its imitator in the same bottle with the same label.) One camouflage technique is simply to mimic the background. Like chameleons, some fish can control their pigment cells, called chromatophores, allowing them to change color. Soles, for example, can control both the color and shade of their skin and the actual color pattern to match the background in which they settle. Swimming among coral rubble, the skin will turn blotchy; resting on a sandy bottom, it will assume a uniform speckled look.

Another technique, known as Batesian mimicry, involves one edible fish's copying another fish that is poisonous or distasteful, and which is therefore largely immune to predation. One of the best-known examples is the pufferfish, a highly toxic marine creature, and the leatherjacket. The pufferfish possesses a powerful nerve poison, tetraodotoxin, which may kill a human in a matter of minutes. The leatherjacket, on the other hand, is a fish with no toxins at all. Its only protection is its remarkable likeness to the pufferfish. In fact, the two are so similar in appearance that predators tend to avoid them both.

Blended into their habitats so well that they are barely discernible, the peacock flounder (far left) and the scorpionfish (left) rank as two of the ocean's best camouflagers. The latter's presence is only betrayed by its eyes and white mouth.

The butterfly fish uses coloration to mislead predators. The fish's false eye distracts predators long enough for it to escape, perhaps with only a few torn tail filaments.

At first glance it appears to be no more than a floating piece of seaweed. But closer examination reveals that the vegetation look-alike is actually the leafy sea dragon, a relative of the sea horse.

Sargassum—named after a Portuguese herb—do indeed float in large rafts in the middle of the Atlantic, though never thickly enough to trap even the smallest sailing ship. And the alga did originate from coastal rockweeds, though it has evolved into a truly pelagic seaweed without holdfasts. Because few animals eat *Sargassum*, the algae may live centuries. Some scientists estimate that some of the original *Sargassum* described by Columbus may still be alive today.

Sargassum lends its name to a lens of warm water floating in the cold west-Atlantic. And over the years, the distant, mysterious Sargasso Sea has spawned many a legend—as the home of sea serpents, as the graveyard of ships trapped in its masses of weed, even as the source of a strange and deadly force that has sent aircraft to their doom. Only recently, with the coming of satellites, has the Sargasso been surveyed and analyzed and accepted as part of the global village.

Nearly the size of the continental United States, the Sargasso Sea turns slowly, trapped by a great gyre of the Gulf Stream. The Sargasso lacks any border with land. It also lacks any cross currents or upwellings to stir its waters. And without upwellings, the waters of the Sargasso are wanting in nutrients. No phytoplankton and zooplankton cloud its crystal-clear waters. This large volume of still water basks in the sun, which increases both its temperature and salinity. Where temperatures in surrounding waters drop to 32°F during the winter, the waters of the Sargasso remain around 64°F. Despite the scarcity of phytoplankton, the warm, salty water supports a variety of life forms, living on and among the tangled masses of *Sargassum*. Sea slugs, swimming crabs 2,000 miles from the nearest rocky shore, shrimp and fish all thrive here, many oddly shaped and cryptically colored to match the mustardy weed rafts.

The sargassum fish especially has adapted wondrously to life in the Sargasso. One of few fish with prehensile fins, it crawls, fin over fin, through the weed mats, hidden both by yellowish blotches and many leafy, frilled tabs of skin. Slow in the weeds, the sargassum fish can switch to jet propulsion in open water, blowing water forcefully out of its gill openings and lurching forward in quick darts. *Sargassum* also provides a nursery for young marlin, swordfish, tuna and flying fish. Then there are the eels.

The life cycle of the eels, both American and European species, proved nearly as baffling as the tales of disappearing ships. In 1856, a German naturalist discovered and described what he believed to be a new fish. He named these small, transparent, leaf-shaped creatures *Leptocephalus*, slender heads. Forty years later, two ichthyologists in Italy, nurturing *Leptocephalus* in an aquarium, were astounded to see them metamorphose into elvers, young European eels. Another ichthyologist spent 20 years tracing leptocephalus (now demoted to a lowercase common name), catching smaller and smaller specimens until he reached the center of the Sargasso, where the specimens averaged only three-tenths of an inch. Later, marine biologists dredged up the pea-sized eggs from 500 feet down.

Eel eggs hatch, and leptocephali float to the surface to join the zooplankton swimming among the *Sargassum*. There they drift, riding first the merry-go-round of the Sargasso itself, and later the Gulf Stream to Europe. The trip may take three years. By the time the larvae near the coast, they have grown to three inches long, but retain their leafy shape and lack of color. Apparently the first hint of fresh water mixing into the salty Atlantic stimulates a remarkable transformation from lep-

Buoyed up by small air bladders, the weed that gives the Sargasso Sea its name floats untethered hundreds of miles from shore. The drifting plant shelters a variety of marine fauna, some of which have evolved a camouflage that blends in perfectly with the feathery clumps. Sparsely scattered throughout the two-and-a-half million square mile Sargasso Sea, the sargassum plant breaks into fragments that flourish separately, some living for centuries.

tocephalus into long, snake-like elvers. The elvers' sense of smell is keen enough to detect a single molecule of odorant introduced into laboratory water, and they seem to use this sense to head for freshwater streams.

A 3,000-mile transatlantic trip is remarkable enough, but once in fresh water, some elvers—mostly female, for unknown reasons—begin another leg of their journey, this time under their own power. Elvers slither over rocks and locks toward their goal in an overwhelming drive to swim upstream. Eels were found 200 miles above the 420-foot dam across the Zambesi River on the Zambesi-Zimbabwe border, 10 years after it was built. Just how they climbed the obstacle no one is quite sure. Some eels swim up the Rhine to an altitude of 3,500 feet, while others negotiate 50 miles of underground passages to show up in Lake Janina in Greece.

Born at the southern edge of the Sargasso Sea, American eels travel the North Equatorial Current and the Gulf Stream to their own streams, a trip only one-third as long. Remarkably, these leptocephali also mature just as they arrive at the coast, perhaps cued by the scent of fresh water rather than age.

Seven to fourteen years after entering fresh water, mature eels head back down stream, toward the sea. Their reproductive organs mature as they migrate; the eels' color changes from yellow-green to metallic silver. Their eyes enlarge and re-tune

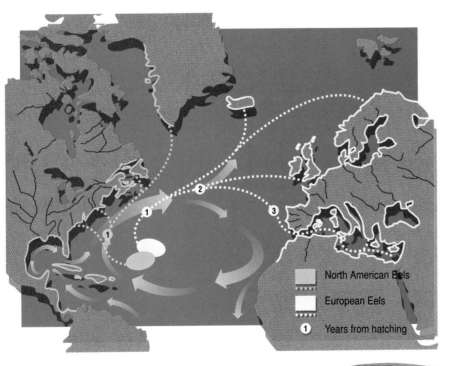

North American Eels

European Eels

① Years from hatching

Two species of eels—European and American—breed in overlapping areas of the Sargasso Sea. After the eggs hatch, they begin a migration that takes them to the rivers and ponds of their ancestors one to three thousand miles away, guided, some biologists believe, by bits of magnetite in their heads that serve as primitive compasses. Riding currents that rim the Sargasso Sea, the elvers metamorphose as they swim, from quarter-inch-long organisms called leptocephalus to full-grown eels that can grow several feet in length (below).

to cope with the wavelengths of light in the ocean. They cease feeding, losing their teeth and eventually their digestive systems. A swim bladder develops to cope with the varying depths they will encounter in the ocean.

After a year (less for American eels) of swimming near the bottom, the sexually mature eels reach their breeding ground somewhere in the Sargasso, probably guided by odor and possibly by a magnetic sense. The females lay from seven million to 13 million eggs; the males spread sperm-containing milt over the eggs; and then the spent parents die. The exact location of eel breeding grounds remains unknown; no adult eel has ever been collected in the open ocean. The remarkable journey of the eels presents a scientific puzzle. Some scientists theorize that ancestral eels bred at a place between North America and Africa when the two continents were only recently separated. As the continents drifted apart over the eons, the eels began migrating, slightly more each century.

HARVESTING THE OCEAN'S BOUNTY

Eels were food long before they became a scientific enigma. Europeans traditionally trap eels as they head downriver. Likewise, seafaring nations around the globe have gathered food from the sea for centuries. In the past, with primitive techniques and a small population to support, fishing barely had begun to tap the rich resources in the ocean. But today, with huge ships crisscrossing the oceans, dragging immense fishing nets and sweeping up tons of cod or tuna at a single stroke, fishing has become far more efficient—perhaps too efficient.

Modern technology has taken much of the guesswork out of finding fish. Whereas in the past, fishermen could gauge the richness of a fishing ground by telltale factors like the color of the water—green meant more plankton and therefore more fish—and seabirds swirling over the ocean's surface, today's fishermen can call upon the resources of the Space Age. Satellite observations allow a wide-angle view unavailable to ships. In two minutes, a satellite scans an area that would take a ship 11 years to cover. The primary instrument used for assessing the oceans is the Coastal Zone Color Scanner, or CZCS. Carried aloft on NASA's Nimbus 7 satellite in 1978 to test the feasibility of measuring ocean color, the original CZCS produced data for seven years beyond its designed lifetime of one year. Three more ocean color scanners are scheduled for launch by the end of the 1990s.

The sensor computes the amount of green light reflected from the ocean, primarily by chlorophyll. Constructing a map made up of thousands of pixels, or picture elements, each of which records a specific level of lightness or darkness, the scanner can accurately locate phytoplankton blooms and busts, current eddies and swirls, and can even measure the temperature by recording infrared light. The satellite and associated computers speak only in numbers, so maps are printed in false colors to enhance contrast.

To make practical use of such maps, NASA broadcasts scans of the Pacific directly to fishing boats by radio. Computers on the boats assemble the data and print a black and white map. With a little time spent painting by number, the captain has an accurate, up-to-the-minute snapshot of the richest fishing grounds.

The CZCS and other high-tech tools are causing most commercial fish to be hunted to capacity; in some areas, such as Antarctica, populations are seriously threatened. Some scientists suggest that expanding humans' menu to include animals such as hake, krill and squid could increase the yearly take six times without overfishing. Others posit that the scheme has serious repercussions—that increasing the harvesting of krill and squid, for example, will merely reduce the amount available to the various sea animals who already depend on those sources.

As fast as people fish, human populations grow faster, and just as hunting gave way to ranching, commercial fishing may yield to marine farming, or aquaculture. Some salmon farms produce 1,000 tons of fish per year. And even seaweed gets into the picture. Algiculture netted nearly $1 billion in Japan in the 1980s.

A variety of mollusks grow well on farms, from the familiar oyster to more exotic conch and giant clam. The most common method of growing oysters is to dangle shells on long ropes in the water. Planktonic oyster larvae settle on the shells and grow. Three hundred farms in protected bays and inlets of southern Japan grow pearl oysters by this method, but spawning oysters artificially and raising them for the table require different techniques. By warming breeding stock, U.S. hatchery managers induce them to release eggs and sperm in tanks. The larvae become almond-sized oysters in eight weeks, then are seeded sparsely on a bay bottom. In three years they are ready to sell on the half shell. Farming Caribbean conch and giant clam, by contrast, remains in experimental stages. The clam, which harbors endosymbiotic algae, grows fast, reaching a market size in a few years.

Fish hatcheries around the world have long raised salmon smolts from milt and eggs to replenish or enhance stream stocks. In a farm, however, smolts by the thou-

A diver inspects the net of a salmon pen in British Columbia, Canada, surrounded by some of its 45,000 residents. Salmon are voracious eaters. A million fish can consume as much as 10 tons of food pellets in a single day. By controlling growing conditions and experimenting with the normal life cycle of fish, aquaculture—the farming of the waters—can produce a much higher yield than regular commercial fishing. Scientists are even experimenting with genetic engineering to produce new, bigger, faster-growing species.

sands live in pens, growing to market size—about six pounds—in a year and a half. Raising up to a million salmon in one small area can create a lot of fish feces, fouling the water. Flushed fiercely twice daily by tides, the Bay of Fundy, between the Canadian provinces of Nova Scotia and New Brunswick, has proved ideal for salmon farms. Strong tides sluice out feces and leftover food, providing excellent pen conditions for about 55 Canadian and U.S. fish farms. Salmon farmers also face the task of feeding their flock. A million salmon can eat 10 tons in a single sunny day, so dry salmon chow is a must. Manufactured in Canada, the fish kibbles include fish meal—or whatever protein source is cheapest at the time—plus oil and several vitamins.

North Americans love salmon, but the same cannot be said of eel. In Japan, however, the slimy-skinned, snake-like fish is a delicacy, and the Japanese consume probably more eel than any other country. Not only have they netted eels for hundreds of years, the Japanese also have farmed them since the late 1800s. After being destroyed during World War II, the industry is rebounding, helped by high-tech controls and indoor tanks. Japanese eels, like their Atlantic cousins, migrate to mysterious mating grounds at sea, so scientists have not succeeded in spawning eels in captivity. Fishermen catch elvers and transport them to farms.

Elvers know what they like, and commercial food served at the surface is definitely not it. They must be taught to eat, by mixing artificial food into fresh, mashed *Tubifex* worms. Gradually increasing the proportion of commercial food, and raising the food tray off the bottom, hatchery workers train the elvers to eat at the sur-

The blue blood that a researcher extracts from horseshoe crabs serves as the basis of an inexpensive test for bacterial contamination. Drugs that fight cancer, viruses and perhaps even AIDS have been extracted from various marine species. Some scientists believe that the oceans ultimately could prove to be a richer source for pharmacologists than tropical rain forests as a source of drugs.

face, where their eating habits can be monitored. Farmed eels grow fast, producing as much as 70,000 pounds per acre per year.

Another important part of aquaculture is seaweed. Japan harvests nearly two dozen edible seaweeds, and some species have been part of the Japanese diet for a millennium. Seaweeds enhance soup, sushi and salad in Japan. Ranchers in Canada and Europe fortify cattle feed with nutritious seaweed meal.

THE OCEAN PHARMACY

While oceans have provided food for humans since the birth of civilization, it is only recently that they have begun supplying a need that may prove equally beneficial. Inspired by decades of successful sampling of tropical plants for drugs that can fight a host of diseases from cancer to colds, marine biologists and drug companies are now investigating ocean organisms in the hopes of finding similarly promising medicines.

Because many marine animals die quickly after being collected, marine pharmacologists often run a battery of tests on board ship. Divers collect a novel specimen and rush it to the surface. There a chemist makes an extract of the tissue and immediately tests it for its effect on the nervous system and against bacteria, viruses or tumors. This shotgun approach is expensive: Only one chemical out of thousands tested ever reaches a clinical test, and the whole process can take a decade or more. Development of a single drug may cost up to $60 million.

Like many drug-producing plants, sea animals often make chemicals to protect themselves. Sponges, which just sit there on the bottom filtering water and waiting for any predator to take a bite, must taste awful. A bite of many sponges would include thousands of spicules, tiny crystalline needles of glass or limestone. Others would feel like shoe leather. Even if a predator could chew the sponge, it might die of the sponge's toxin.

One South Pacific sponge yielded a toxin that kills yeast. With a little chemical modification, it proved effective against vaginal yeast infections. Studying a class of compounds extracted from a Caribbean sponge led researchers to strong antiviral agents expected to fight the cold sore virus and some cancers. Another tropical sponge, this one from the Palau islands in the Pacific yielded a novel, non-narcotic anti-inflammatory agent. Either the chemical itself or a synthetic derivative may prove useful in combating arthritis. These are just a few of the potential drugs derived from sponges. Sea squirts, marine worms and sea whips have all yielded chemicals worthy of further testing. Octopus saliva forms the basis of Eledone, a drug used to fight high blood pressure. Even chemicals from cyanobacteria and algae have been investigated as possible drugs.

A compound derived from herring sperm, though, may turn out to be one of the most important drugs in this half century. Azothymidine, or AZT is the first drug to be approved for extended clinical tests in treating AIDS, acquired immune deficiency syndrome. The early results look promising. AZT kills the virus responsible for AIDS in the test tube, and some improvement has been seen in patients with this invariably fatal disease.

Having helped to nourish the human race for eons, the sea may yet yield its most fruitful crop, curing ailments affecting millions of people, and fighting diseases still not diagnosed.

Window on the Ocean

Beneath its liquid veil, California's Monterey Bay conceals an astonishing variety of marine life. In 1984 some of this watery world was revealed to the landbound public when the $55-million Monterey Bay Aquarium raised it above sea level. By recreating the Bay's thriving habitats so convincingly, the aquarium, home to 525 species, serves as a microcosmic extension of this rich underwater environment.

From octopus to otters, from shellfish to sharks, all of the aquarium's oceanic occupants continue to ply the fresh Monterey sea-water in which some of them were reared. Their water is drawn directly from the bay at a rate of up to 2,050 gallons a minute through two 16-inch-diameter intake pipes. The salty elixir circulates through two big tanks—combined, they contain more than 600,000 gallons of water—and filters into smaller tanks such as those that are home to flatfish, hermit crabs, sand dollars and other sandy-bottom dwellers. By day, the incoming water is filtered to maintain its clarity for public viewing. By night, the filters are shut off so that plankton can enter as the main course for an aquatic feeding frenzy attended by the aquarium's resident invertebrates.

Despite the nutritious supply of seawater, swaying fronds of giant kelp need extra pampering; their health is dependent upon the constant rhythmic motion of the ocean that brings nutrients within reach of their fronds. Hidden atop their three-story-high tank is a pump—resembling a large plunger in a tube—that rocks the 335,000 gallons of kelp forest water in a serene, undulating motion known as surge. The pump's motor drives the plunger upward, sucking water into the

tube, and then downward, pushing the water out, thus creating the surge so vital to kelp.

At the rocky shore exhibit, a mechanically driven wave crashes into the intertidal zone, bathing barnacles, anemones and mollusks living there. Each wave begins as a volume of water contained in a pipe one story above. At regular intervals, a door at the end of the pipe opens to release the built-up water, which crashes down onto the rocks below. A more placid feature of the rocky shores exhibit is the nearby touch tide pool where visitors, under the supervision of guides, can closely inspect—and even touch—star fish, crabs, sea cucumbers and chitons.

Another hands-on exhibit is in the rocky shores gallery, where would-be marine scientists can finger a joystick to guide a macro-lens video camera, track-mounted above the water, through the exhibit. The microscopic action caught by the camera's eye, be it crabs eating or sea slugs mating, can be viewed on screens nearby.

No macro lens is necessary to see the larger life frolicking in the great tide pool. A home-away-from-home for sea otters and harbor seals seeking temporary refuge from the bustle of ocean life, this outdoor pool is visible to the public from an overhanging deck. The rock-ringed pool was built by engineers who used the existing natural rock formations and then added creations of their own design, fabricated of steel and fiberglass-reinforced concrete and, finally, textured and colored to a rock-like finish. As waves wash over the barrier, the great tide pool's residents can come and go as they please, alternately extending the boundaries of both the bay and the aquarium.

Fringing the coast of the bay it so accurately depicts, the 216,000-square-foot Monterey Bay Aquarium is the main attraction of Cannery Row in Monterey, the sardine canning town brought to literary fame by John Steinbeck. The non-profit aquarium, built with funds donated by computer mogul David Packard, is devoted to marine-life research and public education.

Divers plunge daily into the kelp forest to hand-feed some of the larger fish and to perform maintenance and research. The tank is the tallest in the world and the first place where giant kelp, which can grow as much as 14 inches in a day, have been raised successfully in captivity. The tank is roofless for access to air and sun and its acrylic windows are 7 inches thick to withstand 335,000 gallons of water.

SECRETS OF
THE OCEAN FLOOR

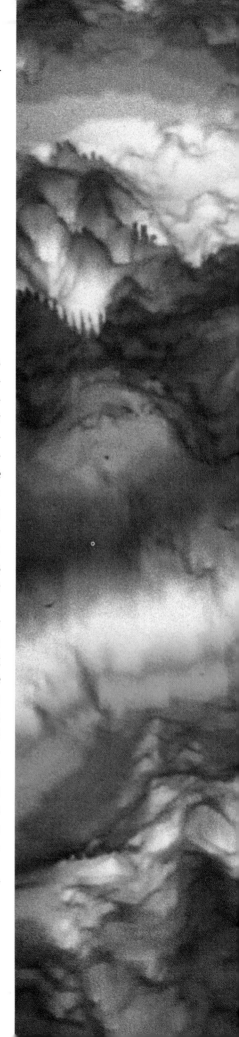

Once it was thought to look like little more than "saucers of great thicknesses of mud in a motionless abyss"—a world both undisturbed and monotonously flat. But today, after several centuries of energetic enterprise and painstaking research, scientists know differently. The ocean floor is an awesomely varied terrain, rivaling anything found on land in its diversity: towering volcanos that rise thousands of feet from the ocean floor; cliffs whose vertiginous pitches are the steepest inclines on the planet and whose drops—sometimes 12,000 feet at a swoop—dwarf the Grand Canyon's mile-high palisades; serpentine canyons 100 miles long, with basalt walls 6,000-feet high; jagged mountain peaks taller than Mount Everest; trenches that plunge tens of thousands of feet into the rock making up the ocean floor; basins of sublime smoothness blanketed by mile-thick sediments. And dominating them all—a chain of volcanoes that stitches a crooked path to form a single, 40,000-mile seam engirdling the globe, the longest mountain range on the planet.

But these are mere glimpses of the submarine terrain; the fundamental character of the world beneath the waves remains but murkily perceived. Bathymetry (from the Greek words *bathys*, for deep, and *metron*, for measure), the science that attempts to chart the features of the ocean floor in much the way geologists have mapped those of dry land, is still in its infancy. Even after half a century of taking accurate depth soundings, only five percent of the topography beneath the seas has been precisely assayed. Incredibly, the surface of Mars, orbiting the Sun 50 million miles from Earth, has been surveyed by interplanetary probes with far greater thoroughness. That may be surprising, but it is not without reason. Despite the fact that it is tantalizingly close, the deep ocean is as inhospitably remote as outer space—a world of stygian darkness and immense pressure that reaches as high as seven tons per square inch. And then there is the sheer magnitude of the terrain: 174 million square miles in all—more than 50 times the size of the con-

This computer-generated map depicts the Atlantic Ocean floor between Africa and South America. The central feature is an 8,000-foot-deep valley, surrounded by mountains of the Mid-Atlantic Ridge. The sea floor—plumbed by modern sonar techniques—has revealed a physiognomy as varied as anything found on land.

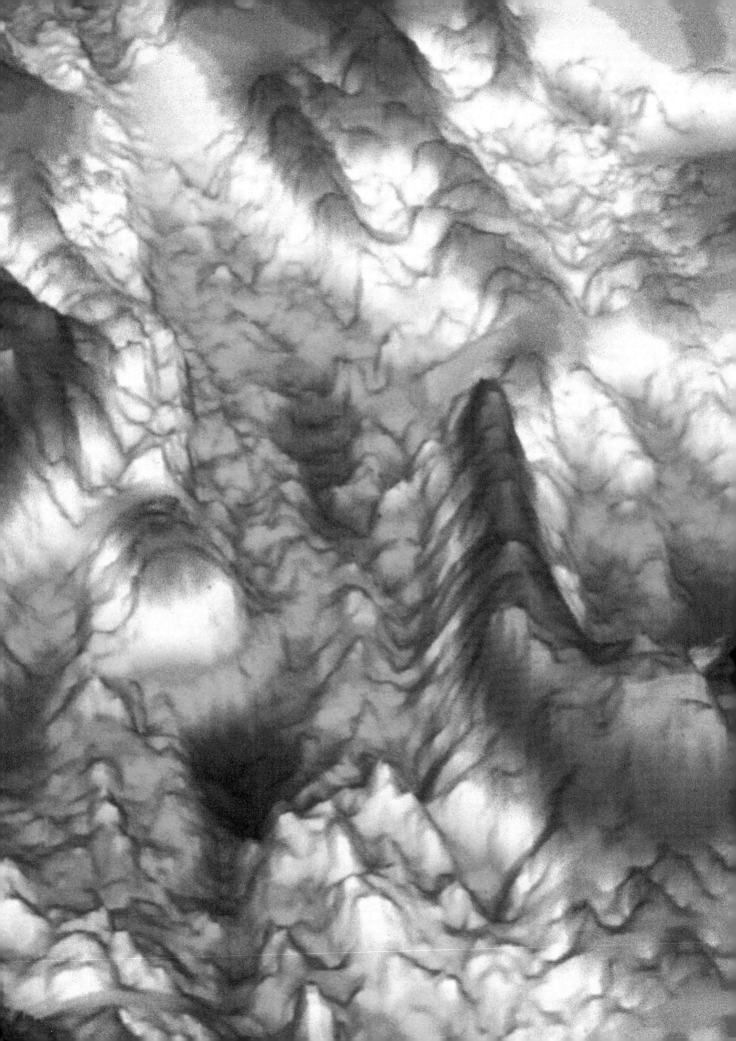

tinental United States. Unlocking the secrets of the ocean floor has occupied scientists for several centuries; it will be several more before the ocean floor's physiognomy has been completely unmasked.

PROBING THE DEPTHS

Navigators and geologists now possess equipment of unmatched power for charting the surface and underwater reaches of the ocean: electronic cameras, computer-assisted sounding devices and research vessels that successfully ply the seven seas. In the past, curious observers confronted the same task with few tools other than a wind-driven ship and their own imagination. In 1521, during his fateful attempt to sail around the globe, the Portuguese explorer Ferdinand Magellan paused near what is now the Polynesian archipelago of Tuamotu to conduct an investigation. Magellan had his crew splice six lengths of rope together and then ordered the resulting line played out in an attempt to probe the Pacific's depths. After 2,500 feet of his makeshift measuring tape had unwound over the side, Magellan decided that the great western ocean was unimaginably profound.

The waters below the craft that day probably stood about 15,000 feet, close to the average depth for the Pacific Basin. But erratic ideas about the extent of all the oceans were promulgated for at least the next three centuries. The 18th-Century astronomer and mathematician Pierre de Laplace calculated the ocean's depth as 12 miles; another investigator pegged it at 23 miles; still others were convinced that the ocean simply was bottomless. Systematic efforts to plumb the oceans began in the early 1800s when Sir John Ross, a British captain, invented a device he named the deep-sea clamm, after the mollusk that inspired it. Effectively an oversized pair of forceps made of cast-iron plates, braced open and fitted with a mechanism that caused it to snap shut when it hit bottom, the clamm (the extra "m" was a 19th-Century version of the modern spelling) hauled up intriguing samples of flora and fauna. Its bathymetric readings, however, were wildly inaccurate. On one occasion the crew paid out 1,050 fathoms (one fathom equals six feet) and assumed that, since the line ran vertically down the ship, the clamm had finally struck bottom. But when the line was retrieved, a floor-dwelling starfish was found attached at the 800-fathom mark. More than 200 fathoms of line must have been lying on the sea floor.

By 1840, Sir John's nephew, James Ross, paused in the South Atlantic during a voyage to the Antarctic to take the first true sounding of the deep ocean using hemp fed from a spool and attached to a lead weight of 72 pounds. A few days later, a second sounding was made using a 540-pound weight. Modern scientists speculate that the younger Ross's readings, which consistently exceed modern ones, were skewed by the fact that his thick line continued unrolling, dragged downward by its own weight, even after the lead plummets had struck bottom. In 1845, five years after Ross conducted his soundings, an American naval officer, Matthew Fontaine Maury, devised a method that proved to be more accurate. In the process, he was able to create a generalized bathymetric chart of the entire North Atlantic. Maury carried out his measurements with 60-pound-test twine, marked at 100-fathom, or 600-foot, intervals and attached to either a 32- or 68-pound cannonball. During soundings, sailors carefully monitored the playing out of the twine, and when the rate at which the twine was uncoiling slowed markedly,

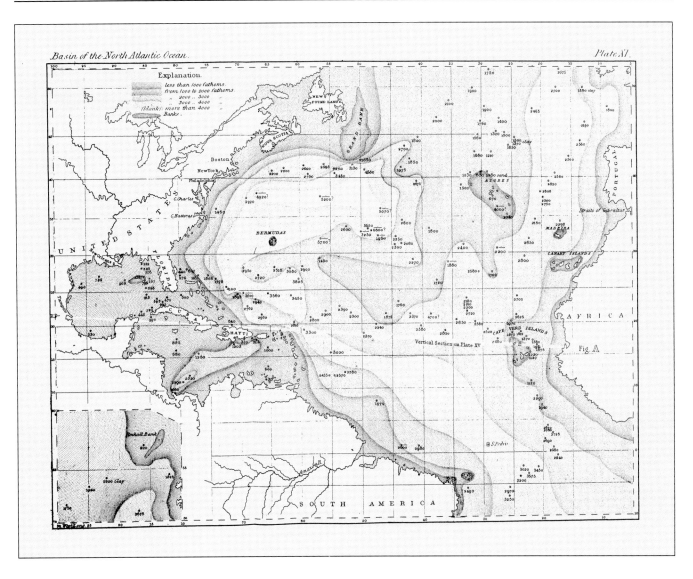

Basin of the North Atlantic Ocean.   Plate XI.

PLUMBING THE DEPTHS

Published in The Physical Geography of the Sea *in 1854, this map of the basin of the North Atlantic was the first detailed chart that showed the depth of the ocean. The map's creator, Lieutenant Matthew Fontaine Maury, took 150 soundings deeper than 6,000 feet and then extrapolated to produce a topographical map of the ocean floor. Although primitive and misleading by modern standards, the map gave an inkling of the varied face of the ocean floor.*

assumed that its cannonball had touched ground. By 1854, Maury had produced a useful but somewhat rough rendering of the North Atlantic, plotting 150 soundings that were deeper than 1,000 fathoms and then filling in the sketchy ground between by extrapolation.

Taking just one deep-sea reading in this primitive fashion could eat up an entire day, since the line had to be hauled in hand over hand. By the 1870s, the task had been eased somewhat by the introduction of steam-driven winches, which cut hours off the chore. With this mechanical aid, the H.M.S. *Challenger* expedition, launched from England in 1872 on a three-and-a-half-year, round-the-world cruise, plumbed the waters of every ocean but the Arctic, and gathered enough data over one 140-square-mile section of the Atlantic to draft a detailed map. *Challenger*'s expedition provided enough data to eventually fill 50 large volumes written by 76 authors; the voyage marked the beginning of modern oceanography.

Despite further refinements in the 1880s, in which piano wire replaced bulky ropes and enabled navigators to execute several soundings per day, the traditional means of charting the ocean floor remained time-consuming and clumsy. But in 1914, a protegé of American inventor Thomas Alva Edison perfected a device that

SEEING WITH SOUND

Oceanographers use sound waves to "see" the ocean floor and to determine its depth. Modern sonar mapping systems can use both multibeam and side-look systems. Multi-beam is an array of hull-mounted sound-emitters that send a band of low-frequency sound signals toward the ocean floor. The signals hit the floor, bounce back to the surface and are recorded by receivers called hydrophones, also mounted to the hull. By knowing the speed that sound travels in water and timing each signal, computer-aided scientists can determine the depth of the floor with an accuracy of a few feet and produce three-dimensional images of its topography.

More detailed textural data is gathered by a side-look sonar system. Like multibeam, this system is comprised of an array of sound-emitters and hydrophone receivers; unlike multibeam, side-look sonar is a vehicle towed beneath the surface. The system is called "side-look" because it looks at the floor with sound waves transmitted from the side of the device. A swath of signals is projected from each side of the vehicle on an angle directed toward the floor. Instead of measuring the signal's travel time for depth only, the return signal also is measured for its intensity, which reveals the floor's relief and textural qualities as well.

Ocean floor mappers must cope with a range-for-resolution tradeoff. For deep-water sounding, low-frequency sound waves are used because they travel farther than high-frequency waves and therefore can penetrate greater depths and cover a larger area. However, high frequency waves have better powers of resolution and are used when it is necessary to discern fine detail.

GLORIA
An acronym for Geological Long-Range Inclined Asdic, GLORIA is a shallow-towed system, dragged a few hundred yards below the surface. Both a conventional side-scan sonar and bathymetric (depth) mapping system, GLORIA produces an ocean floor image up to 40 miles wide. Towed at 10 knots, it can cover 2,500 square nautical miles a day—an area roughly one-third the size of Vermont.

Tow ship
Carries a row of sound-emitting and receiving instruments, called multibeam sonar, mounted on its hull, to measure relief and the exact distance to the ocean floor. The towed sonar devices are lowered into the water off the ship's fantail from a boat-trailer-like carriage, which rolls along the deck on golf-cart tires.

Tow cable
Provides power to the side-look sonar and allows it to be towed through the water. Kevlar-strengthened, the cable also transmits information gleaned by the side-look sonar devices back to the ship.

SeaMARC I side-look sonar
Towed close to the ocean floor, SeaMARC I (Sea Mapping and Remote Characterization) sends out high-frequency sound waves at an angle and measures their return time, in water as deep as 30,000 feet. Used in conjunction with multibeam sonar, side-look sonar can provide fine textural details as well as a contour map of the ocean floor.

Width of coverage
2 miles

2.5 miles

Width of coverage
18 miles

Width of coverage
4 miles

Depressor
Attached to the tow cable to dampen the effects of the ship in rough seas, this one-ton weight also serves as a sinker to keep the sonar devices, also known as the "fish," at their proper towing height.

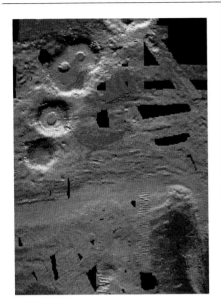

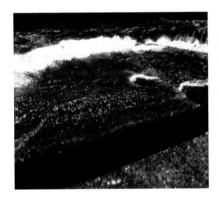

SONAR MAPS

The top ocean-floor image was made using a multibeam sonar and reveals a 25-mile-wide swath of the axis of the East Pacific Rise, just south of the Clipperton Fracture Zone at the top of the image. The shallowest depths, about 5,500 feet, are white; the deepest, about 10,000 feet, are dark blue. The image at bottom was made using the SeaMARC I side-looking sonar, and reveals only part of the large caldera, or crater, but with greater resolution than on the multibeam image. The swath here is 1.2 miles wide and shows the steep caldera wall, almost 1,000 feet high, in the background and smaller pit craters on the floor of the main crater.

revolutionized bathymetry. Galvanized by the sinking of the *Titanic* two years before, Reginald Fessenden employed acoustical, rather than physical, feelers to locate objects—whether icebergs like the one that destroyed the *Titanic*, other ships or dangerous shoals.

Earlier navigators had realized that it might be possible to sense submerged obstacles by monitoring the way in which sounds echoed through the water; they actually had used hammers to beat the hulls of their ships so that the noises might bounce off hidden hazards. Fessenden's approach was to mount a doorbell-like ringer on a ship's hull. The steadily emitted sound waves from the ringer sped through the water (sound travels a mile each second under water—five times faster than in air), bounced off obstacles, and were returned to the ship, where they were picked up by an underwater microphone called a hydrophone. Inside the ship, a technician listening to the echoes could detect tonal shifts that signaled the presence of an object in the ship's path. In practice, this so-called echo-location, which literally sounds the depths, mimics the faculty that permits bats to fly at night and porpoises to negotiate coastal waters.

Fessenden's instrument was dubbed sonar, an acronym for Sound Navigation and Ranging, and was intended to be aimed sideways from the ship to detect obstructions on the ocean's surface. A German scientist, Alexander Behm, quickly turned sonar to bathymetric purposes by shifting the signaling downward, toward the sea floor. By timing how long it took for a single ping to make the round trip from the ship to the sea floor and back, then dividing by two, it was possible to arrive at the distance the sound waves had traveled, and therefore the depth of the water. During World War II, sonar served a vital role by detecting the presence of submarines, helping protect Allied ships from surprise attacks.

Since the 1950s, sonar devices have grown ever more sophisticated. Modern equipment generates sound waves with exquisite precision by using materials whose atomic structures cause them to oscillate and emit sound waves when they are subjected to certain stimuli. Certain crystals—quartz is one example—will react to alternating electrical currents by sending out a series of ultrasonic pings. Since these crystals—known as piezoelectric substances—also work in reverse, producing electricity when they are struck by sound waves, they do double duty in modern sonar devices. Not only do they act as sound generators; they also serve as sensors, converting the returning echoes to impulses that feed into sensitive timing and recording instruments.

Oceanographers now depend on two main versions of sonar: side-looking—also known as side-scanning—and multibeam. The former device, introduced in 1957, is towed beneath and behind a ship at speeds of up to 10 knots. The apparatus normally consists of a small box of acoustic and electronic instruments and a set of buoyant spheres, all contained in a sturdy torpedo-shaped "tow-fish." As it is pulled along underwater, sound waves issue and rebound below and on either side of the device. The echoes register on hydrophones, which transmit the information via a Kevlar-strengthened cable to the mother ship, where it is processed by computer and may be translated into a running graphic display called a sonograph. The sonograph, built up line by line, presents an almost photographic likeness of the submarine terrain. Side-look sonar is either shallow-towed or deep-towed. The former covers a wider swath and gives a picture analogous to a bird's-eye view. With deep towing, the "fish" can skim closely and slowly over the ocean floor, looking sideways as well as down, and giving better resolution.

Multibeam sounders, which made their debut in the 1960s, differ from side-scanners in that the instruments are not towed but mounted on the ship's hull. The sound emitters run along, and the hydrophones across, the keel. Hull-mounted sonar looks down and out at the sea floor. However, rather than processing the echoes into a photo-like image, these sonars divide the echoes into multiple beams to ensure precise depths. The densely spaced depths are combined by computer to form a contour map of the ocean floor.

Working in tandem, side-looking and multibeam sonar can generate not only a contour map of the ocean floor, but also can provide finely detailed textural information, revealing the "grass in the rough and on the green, and the sand in the bunker," as one golfing scientist puts it. The quality of the images is a delight to oceanographers—and a source of concern for others. The results of detailed mapping of the United States' Exclusive Economic Zone—a 200-nautical-mile band of water that surrounds the U.S. and its territories—was long kept under wraps. American military officials were concerned that the charts could help the crews of enemy submarines pinpoint their exact positions in the oceans—essential in targeting U.S. landbased missile silos. Scientists and military officials have compromised: only certain sensitive areas are kept under wraps.

A VAST AND VARIED WORLD

This composite illustration contains a mixture of features found in the Atlantic and Pacific oceans—soaring mountains, extinct volcanoes, serpentine canyons. The ocean floor is a world of its own, a wildly diverse terrain obscured until recently by water often several miles deep. Modern sonar has stripped away the briny shroud and exposed the ocean floor topography; in doing so, sonar has helped scientists understand the genesis of oceans.

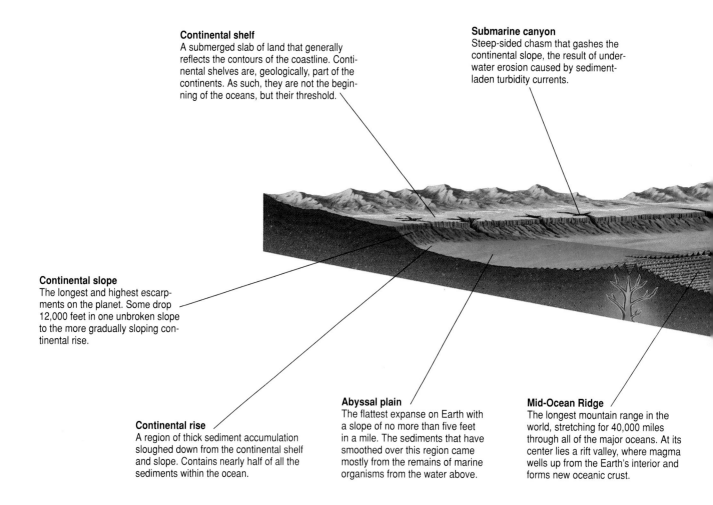

Continental shelf
A submerged slab of land that generally reflects the contours of the coastline. Continental shelves are, geologically, part of the continents. As such, they are not the beginning of the oceans, but their threshold.

Submarine canyon
Steep-sided chasm that gashes the continental slope, the result of underwater erosion caused by sediment-laden turbidity currents.

Continental slope
The longest and highest escarpments on the planet. Some drop 12,000 feet in one unbroken slope to the more gradually sloping continental rise.

Continental rise
A region of thick sediment accumulation sloughed down from the continental shelf and slope. Contains nearly half of all the sediments within the ocean.

Abyssal plain
The flattest expanse on Earth with a slope of no more than five feet in a mile. The sediments that have smoothed over this region came mostly from the remains of marine organisms from the water above.

Mid-Ocean Ridge
The longest mountain range in the world, stretching for 40,000 miles through all of the major oceans. At its center lies a rift valley, where magma wells up from the Earth's interior and forms new oceanic crust.

A VARIEGATED SEASCAPE

Before World War II, the results of the soundings taken around the world gradually found their way to a single, unprepossessing office in Monaco, where an agent of the International Hydrographic Bureau dutifully recorded the information on the comprehensive *Carte générale bathymétrique du monde*, or World Bathymetric Map. In this way, a portrait of the ocean basins was assembled, point by laborious point. The explosion of data that took place after the perfection of deep-sea sonar ended forever this quaint—and unreliable—enterprise. It also recast man's understanding of the ocean basins and how they fit into the overall scheme of the planet's ongoing geological evolution.

The floor of the sea is subject to powerful forces that act to shape it from above and below; as a consequence an ocean basin such as the Atlantic exhibits as varied a terrain as any continental landmass. Extending out from the shoreline is a gently sloping plain known as the continental shelf. Although under water, the continental shelf does not belong to the ocean basins; geologically, it is a submerged part of the continent. In some places around the rim of the Atlantic, the continental shelf narrows to fewer than 10 miles, but elsewhere—off the coasts of Newfoundland, Argentina and Northern Europe—it pushes hundreds of miles out to sea.

Currently, 20 percent of the land area of the continents lies submerged on these shelves, a figure that has fluctuated markedly over the millennia. During the most

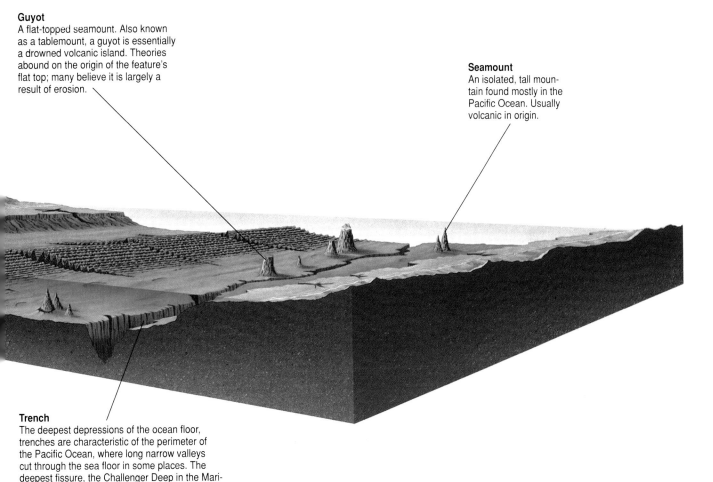

Guyot
A flat-topped seamount. Also known as a tablemount, a guyot is essentially a drowned volcanic island. Theories abound on the origin of the feature's flat top; many believe it is largely a result of erosion.

Seamount
An isolated, tall mountain found mostly in the Pacific Ocean. Usually volcanic in origin.

Trench
The deepest depressions of the ocean floor, trenches are characteristic of the perimeter of the Pacific Ocean, where long narrow valleys cut through the sea floor in some places. The deepest fissure, the Challenger Deep in the Marianas Trench near Guam, is seven miles deep.

Bridging the Continents Underseas

The simplicity of dialing overseas, or rather underseas, belies the complexity of laying call-carrying cables. In fact, it was not until 1956 that a transatlantic cable made the first of such calls even possible. Despite the proliferation of communications satellites since then, 50 percent of all intercontinental phone calls are still being transmitted by undersea cable. Every day, two million calls pass through more than 150,000 miles of cable.

Before laying the cables, engineers consult ocean floor maps to select a potential route and survey it extensively with sonar to determine precise floor depths and relief. They also measure the water's currents, temperature and pressure—forces that can make or break submarine cable.

When the route is deemed acceptable, the cable is hooked to a small ship from a cable station on shore and then pulled seaward. To protect the cable from being snagged or dragged by fishing nets and lobster traps, a device called Sea Plow buries the cable in any water that is less than 4,500 feet deep. In depths beyond that, the cable simply sinks and rests on the bottom. Once past the continental shelf, a larger cable-laying ship, with hundreds of miles of cable coiled in its hull, takes over. The cable is spliced together and the new carrier continues on its way. As if on an ever-extending leash, the ship plies its course at up to eight knots while cable unravels from below deck, snaking up and through a chute at the stern before slinking overboard. Left on its own, the heavy cable would pay itself out much too fast. It must be held back by a linear cable engine, two motorized conveyor belts that sandwich the cable and guide it horizontally to the chute, controlling its pay-out to match the ship's speed. If the length of cable on board falls short of the route's distance, the leading end is buoyed while the ship returns to port to restock cable.

At 90-mile intervals, a device called a repeater passes through the conveyor belts, like an egg swallowed by a snake. Spliced into the cable beforehand, this unit regenerates the telephone signals, which otherwise would weaken as they move along the cable at the speed of light.

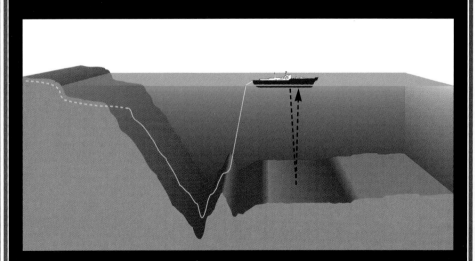

DROPPING THE LINE

As spliced segments of telephone cable are dropped along a previously surveyed route, the crew sounds the floor for immediate depth readings to ensure that they are following the proper course. Knowledge of the floor's depth is necessary to determine how much cable to pay out every step of the way. If too little cable is let out it may become taut and strained; too much cable may coil. Both scenarios can result in later damage to the cable.

The C.S. Global Link (above) is the world's most technically advanced cable laying and repair vessel. Owned by American Telephone and Telegraph, the 16,400-ton ship holds three spool-like cable tanks with 4,100 miles of submarine cable in her hull. The ship's hull is equipped with both bow and stern thrusters that maneuver the ship and help maintain her stability in winds of up to 40 miles per hour.

Traveling along the ocean floor, a machine called Sea Plow carves a three-foot-deep trench into the floor with a cutting disc and a plowshare. The device displaces a wedge of cut floor sideways, guides the cable to the trench and replaces the wedge. Sea Plow can be towed behind a cable-laying ship, burying cable as it is paid out, or it can bury the cable later, guided by a support vehicle or a diver.

recent Ice Age, 10,000 years ago, when an enormous volume of water was locked up in glaciers in the form of ice, the sea level dropped substantially and, as a result, a much greater area of the shelves was exposed. In some cases, regions now separated by water—Alaska and Siberia, for instance—were connected. Millions of years earlier, in a warmer period, there was less polar ice and, therefore, more water; the sea level surged, swallowing half of the North American continent and creating continental shelves thousands of miles wide.

Geologists once thought that the broad, flat terraces fringing the continents had been cut by waves. While a few shelves have been sculpted in this way, others, such as the shelves off Nova Scotia and Maine, are the product of glacial scouring. During the last Ice Age, massive glaciers slid south across the dry shelves to the sea, carving the topography as they passed and leaving behind jumbled loads of rock and gravel. Still other shelves bear smooth, thick layers of mud, silt, clay, or gravel eroded from inland landforms by rivers and deposited along the continental verge in great, alluvial fans.

The boundary of the continental shelves is marked by a precipitous drop known as the continental slope. Often falling off at a rate of from 100 to 500 feet—and sometimes as much as 1,000 feet—per mile, these scarps average 12,000 feet in height and as a class qualify as the longest, highest cliffs on Earth. In one place on the west coast of South America where there is no continental shelf, the drop-off from the top of the Andes Mountains to the bottom of the offshore Peru-Chile Trench traverses 42,000 vertical feet in a 100-mile-long decline.

Here and there, the faces of the continental slopes are breached by great, V-shaped clefts called submarine canyons. Several of these underwater gorges punctuate the continental slope along the Eastern Seaboard of the U.S., including the Hudson and Baltimore canyons. Since these almost always appear beyond the mouths of large rivers, scientists long assumed that the canyons were simply drowned river valleys. But since many canyons snake deeper than 400 feet, far beyond the point past which sea level has fallen in recent geological time, geologists have been forced to search for additional explanations.

Most researchers now agree that powerful underwater streams, called turbidity currents, carve such canyons. Turbidity currents are sometimes extensions of the so-called long-shore currents that flow along the margins of continents, carrying eroded beach material. Over centuries, the coursing of these silt-laden currents cuts into the continental shelf material, creating a conduit that siphons increasingly larger volumes of material seaward. At times, instabilities on the canyon faces develop, leading to sudden slumps and slides that tumble downslope like avalanches, gathering speed and material. Striking evidence of the amount of raw power unleashed in such slides came in 1929, when an earthquake off the Grand Banks south of Newfoundland triggered a slide that snapped transatlantic telegraph cables along a 300-mile path, knocking each cable out of service in domino fashion. Timing the loss of service down the line, scientists deduced that the material at the head of the stream had attained speeds of 25 to 60 miles per hour.

Eventually, the material eroded from canyons and carried by turbidity currents winds up at the continental slope, where it fans out like a delta at the mouth of a river. It may also course onward, cutting a channel down the gradual decline of a feature called—in what seems a misnomer—the continental rise. Thick with

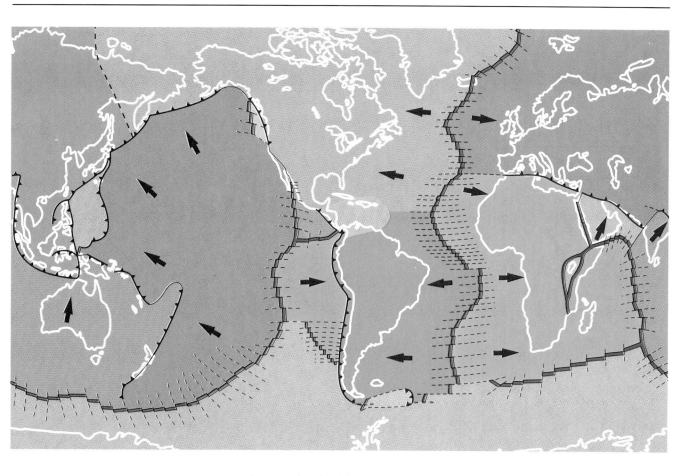

A PUZZLE IN MOTION

All the world's oceans and continents are embedded in a dozen or so rigid plates—portrayed here in different colors—that float on a partially molten layer known as the asthenosphere. The plates, 30 to 90 miles thick, drift at varying speeds and in different directions. Plates moving apart are indicated by arrows; small triangles show where plates collide, such as along the western edge of the Pacific.

sediments sloughed from above, the continental rise marks a more gradual descent than the continental slope, losing about one vertical foot for every 100 horizontal feet. Ranging, in the Atlantic Ocean, from 62 to 620 miles wide, the rise represents the true boundary of the deep ocean basin. Beyond lie the abyssal plains, at depths of 15,000 to 20,000 feet. These occupy 40 percent of the Atlantic and close to half of the Pacific and Indian basins.

The Atlantic plains hold sediment blankets that are up to two miles thick, and as a result appear exceedingly flat and unperturbed; the less-sedimented plains of the Pacific, however, are a jumble of cracks and rugged features. This variety is typical of the other regions of the Pacific. It boasts more diversity of terrain than the Atlantic and has features rarely found in other oceans—underwater volcanoes called seamounts and submarine trenches. Seamounts, formed of the same, once-molten rock type as the ocean floor, are strewn across the central and northern Pacific. The Emperor Seamounts northwest of Hawaii, the Midway Islands to the east, and the Hawaiian Islands themselves all fall into this category. Like the Emperor chain, which has subsided beneath the surface, the other seamounts of this trio, the youngest of which is the million-year-old island of Hawaii, eventually will return to the sea.

Guyots, which already have made the round trip from below the water to above and back, dot the Pacific Basin; more than 10,000 have been discovered. These flattened mounds are volcanic in nature. But it is unclear whether their pointed tops were lost by relentless pounding of waves at the surface, or through some other process, perhaps the construction of ever-widening coral reefs on their tops.

Far and away the most impressive element of either the Pacific or the Atlantic is the feature named the Mid-Ocean Ridge. The 500-mile-wide portion called the Mid-Atlantic Ridge wends its way through the ocean, zigging and zagging before hooking around Cape Horn and entering the Indian Ocean, from where it continues on its 40,000-mile globe-circling way. The mountainous ridge rises on average 10,000 feet above the sea floor, but occasionally—such as at Iceland—juts to the surface. Whereas terrestrial mountains, which are built of sediments that have been subjected to massive pressure, folding and upthrust, can be considered local features, the Mid-Atlantic Ridge and its counterpart in the Pacific, the East Pacific Rise, are global features, representing colossal bulges in the mantle of the Earth. Wracked by earthquakes and eruptions and riven by fissures, the mid-ocean ridges qualify as the most active zones on the planet. In the 1970s, the tiny submersibles *Cyana*, *Archimède* and *Alvin* cruised the centermost clefts of the ridges, called rift valleys, for a joint U.S.-French project called FAMOUS (French-American Mid-Ocean Undersea Study). They scouted a landscape bristling with long, gnarled tubes of rock dubbed "toothpaste lava" and pillow-like rocks that defied explanation. Younger than the continents, and always adding new material, the rift zones hold the key to many geologic mysteries, including how oceans are created.

THE BIRTH AND GROWTH OF OCEANS

During the 1960s and 1970s, evidence mounted that neither the ocean basins nor the continents were immutably fixed, but were constantly shifting. It became clear that over hundreds of millions of years, the physiognomy of the planet had been altered, scrambled by the forces unleashed at the mid-oceanic ridges.

In the 1950s, Princeton geologist Harry Hess had discovered and elucidated a process subsequently called sea floor spreading. Compiling data on the age of rocks from the ocean floors, Hess discovered no record of rocks older than 150 million years. This struck Hess as odd, since some continental rocks dated back billions of years. Evidently, a mechanism existed for adding fresh rock to the ocean basins. Hess guessed that this material issued from the Mid-Ocean Ridge. He postulated that as magma rose from the interior of the Earth, the sea floor on either side fell away from the central rift. In effect, Hess said, the halves of the sea floor resemble huge conveyor belts that head off in opposite directions. When the spreading ocean crust eventually reaches a barrier—the edge of a continent—it is forced back down into the mantle where it is remelted. And so the process continues—new ocean crust being created, older crust being destroyed and recycled.

Elaborating on the concept of sea floor spreading in the 1960s, two young British researchers, Frederick Vine and Drummond Matthews, proposed a comprehensive theory that eventually explained the process behind both the birth and death of oceans. Called plate tectonics (from the Greek *tekton*, "to build"), the theory posited that the Earth's upper mantle and crust—known as the lithosphere—is broken into a dozen or so large and small rigid segments called plates. The plates jostle, occasionally crashing against one another, like gigantic floes in a frozen sea. The continents and ocean are embedded in these plates, which are adrift on the mantle underneath. Sometimes part of an ocean and a continent sit on the same plate; sometimes an ocean sits astride several plates. The rearranging of the lithosphere reflects events deep within the Earth's mantle, where

Tsunami—The Deadly Wave

Although tsunamis (from the Japanese *tsu*—harbor—and *nami*—wave) are frequently referred to as tidal waves, the term is, in fact, a misnomer. The roots of a tsunami lie beneath the oceans. A sudden vertical displacement of the sea floor, occasionally the result of a severe earthquake along the boundary of one of the Earth's plates, releases energy that forms a wave on the ocean's surface.

Traveling at speeds of up to 500 miles per hour, a tsunami moves fastest in deep water, where its wavelength may measure 100 miles between crests. Although popular mythology has characterized these maritime juggernauts as huge mountains of water hurtling through the oceans, in fact they go unnoticed by ships even when they are only a few miles from shore. It is not until tsunamis begin to "feel bottom" close to land that they build up into waves sometimes 100 feet high. They crash onto land with awesome force. A tsunami created by the Great Alaskan Earthquake of March 28, 1964 picked up a number of 50- to 100-foot-long king crab boats in Kodiak, Alaska, and threw them several blocks inland. Five hours later, 2,000 miles away in Crescent City, California, cars floated down inundated streets as the wave struck there. Two hundred homes and business establishments were destroyed.

Such destructive waves are now monitored by the Geostationary Operational Environmental Satellite (GOES), which can detect signals from delicate tide sensors located on platforms in the ocean. If the water level rises beyond a certain point, an electronic message is transmitted to GOES, which in turn flashes the message to a ground station. Tsunami warnings are then sent to the appropriate areas.

The Fault of It All
A sudden vertical faulting on the ocean floor—caused by plate motion or submarine avalanches—results in a displacement of water that reaches the ocean's surface as one- or two-foot-high waves. These waves then radiate; when they near land, they build up into rolling mountains of water that strike shore with awesome force.

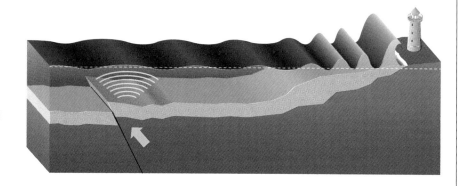

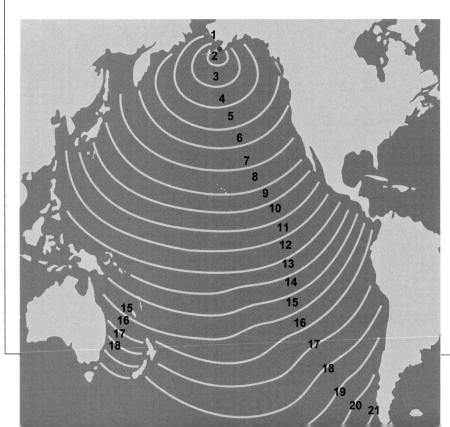

Radiating Destruction
This illustration charts the time it would take for a tsunami that originates off the coast of Alaska to reach various parts of the Pacific Ocean. Tsunamis can traverse 1,000 miles of ocean in little more than two hours.

EARTH'S STIRRING CRUST

The driving force behind the movement of the rigid plates that make up Earth's outer shell is thermal convection, which causes molten rock to rise from the interior to the Earth's surface, where it cools and then descends. Convection can be demonstrated by putting a pan of water over heat. Heat causes the water at the bottom to expand and become less dense; as a result, it rises to the surface, then cools. The density increases again and the water sinks.

Some scientists believe that the convection of magma occurs throughout the entire mantle, extending 1,800 miles beneath the Earth's surface. Others theorize that the currents in the mantle occur in two zones, one extending from the surface down to the depths of the deepest earthquakes—about 400 miles—and another zone that extends from there to the core-mantle boundary.

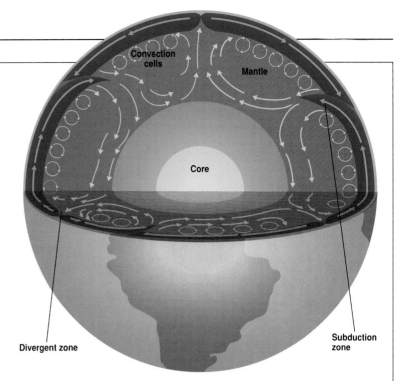

Divergent zone
One of three main types of plate boundaries, a divergent zone is a belt along which plates move apart and magma wells up from the Earth's interior forming new oceanic crust. Mid-ocean ridges, like the one that runs through the center of the Atlantic Ocean, are divergent zones.

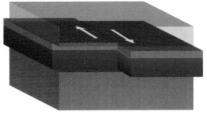

Transform fault
Two jostling plates can slide past each other along a transform fault. Often they are the source of earthquakes. California's famed San Andreas fault, where the Pacific plate slides past the American plate, is such a boundary.

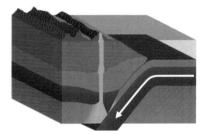

Subduction zone
When plates collide, one usually buckles and slides underneath the other. The subducting plate descends into the hot mantle, where parts of it are melted; deep ocean trenches occur in these areas.

trapped heat sets the mantle's melted rock stirring. Material within the mantle rises and falls like the roiling cells in a pot of boiling soup. In this convection process, magma gathers in vast underground reservoirs one to four miles beneath the Mid-Ocean Ridge. As the tension pulling the Earth apart at the rift mounts, the rock fractures, causing earthquakes and allowing the light, now-molten lava to ascend to the sea floor.

One geologist has called the Mid-Ocean Ridge a "wound that never heals," since it continually oozes the material that forms new oceanic crust. In geologic terms, the rate of accretion is rapid, with the sea floors gaining anywhere from one to seven inches each year. The Atlantic Ridge grows more slowly, spreading an average 1.2 inches annually, while the East Pacific Rise clicks along at an average of 4.7 inches, about twice as fast as a fingernail grows. As well as being the birthing spot of new ocean floor, the Mid-Ocean Ridge also may give rise to various prominences. Some researchers have suggested that flat-topped guyots were originally volcanoes created at ridges. As sea floor spreading carried them steadily away from the ridges, they were severed from their magma source. Deprived of a constant supply of lava, the volcanoes fell into an inevitable geological decline. The basalt of which they are made, though it appears to be dense rock, actually erodes rapidly. Having once lost their tops, the volcanoes continue to be eroded.

Inevitably, material added at these mid-oceanic ridges eventually reaches the edges of the tectonic plates. There a contest sometimes ensues between the oceanic crust, composed of basalt, and the continental crust, composed of granite. Because the oceanic plate is denser, it must take the only path open to it, plunging under the less-dense continental plate and back into the mantle in a process called subduction. But when two plates carrying continental material meet this way, the material buckles, creating ranges such as the Himalayas, which were upthrust in an ancient collision between the plates carrying the Indian subcontinent and Asia.

Great violence accompanies subduction as one plate forces itself under another. So ferocious is the activity around the Pacific Basin that its rim has been called the Ring of Fire. The deep submarine trenches where subduction occurs are punished by earthquakes, caused by the energy released when the rock slides into the mantle. Subduction zones also seethe with volcanic activity. As the sheet of oceanic rock sinks into the hot mantle, it remelts and rises to the surface of the ocean floor in long plumes. The result is a series of related volcanoes lined up somewhat behind, and parallel to, the subduction zone. Examples include the Aleutian Island arc off Alaska and the terrestrial volcanoes in the Cascade Range along the west coast of the U.S., the most notable of which in recent years has been Washington State's fiery Mount Saint Helens.

Researchers also have identified other types of volcano-building plumes that carry material from deep in the mantle and well up in the middle of tectonic plates. The isolated plumes may persist for tens of millions of years, remaining stationary with regard to the moving ocean floor. New volcanoes emerge, grow and then die hundreds of thousands of years later as they are transported off the hot spot by the sliding ocean crust. The Hawaiian Islands owe their existence to such a hot spot, and there are signs that a new addition to the Hawaiian chain, the Loihi Seamount, is already birthing in the warm ocean waters south of Honolulu.

UNLOCKING THE SECRETS

This modern theory of plate tectonics grew out of the work of a German earth scientist, Alfred Wegener, who proposed in 1915 that the continents drifted about the surface of the planet. Looking at maps, Wegener noticed that the continents of South America and Africa fit together neatly like a giant jigsaw puzzle. He suggested that this was not coincidental, but that all the continents had once been a single landmass he dubbed Pangaea, from the Latin meaning "one Earth." Wegener saw proof for this in such phenomena as truncated mountain ranges, which began in South Africa and ended in Argentina, or in fossils found in Africa and again across the waters in Brazil. In hundreds, if not thousands, of cases, field researchers working on continents separated by vast expanses of water exhumed fossil rocks bearing the imprints of identical species. *Glossopteris* ferns, for instance, showed up in India and again in Australia. Also, the remains of plants and animals known to flourish only in tropical zones often appeared in rock samples taken from regions where a temperate climate prevailed.

The Red Ocean?

Given time—in the realm of millions of years—the present-day Red Sea may become the world's next ocean. This possibility rests with three of the dozen or so rigid plates that form the lithosphere—the crust and part of the upper mantle that comprise Earth's outermost shell. Like great rafts, these tectonic plates drift, carrying the continents and oceans that are embedded within them. New plates are created and old plates destroyed in an ongoing geological tale that continually reshapes Earth's physiognomy.

When a plate splits, a new ocean basin is created. The process is thought to begin when the molten rock called magma, welling up from deep within the Earth, weakens and thins the surface crust. If the crust fractures on both sides of a stressed area and crustal spreading begins, sections of it drop, forming a rift valley that later may be inundated by water. (In fact, the Red Sea is part of the East African Rift System that gashes the eastern side of Africa for 3,500 miles.) If the rifting is severe enough, a continent may be

split. The same process, which started 200 million years ago as North America and Europe were severed, created the Atlantic. The two continents are still drifting apart.

A quick glance at a map shows that if the Red Sea were closed, Africa and Saudi Arabia would fit together almost perfectly. Originally, the Arabian Peninsula was part of Africa. But the pulling apart of three plates—the African, Arabian and Somali plates—has allowed the sea to invade the ever-widening gap at the ponderous pace of one-half inch per year.

Whether the plates will continue to separate depends on the tectonic activity in the Afar Triangle, the area where the three plates meet. If the crack continues to widen, the Somali plate will break away from the African continent—as the island of Madagascar did 165 million years ago—and float into the Indian Ocean. But if crustal spreading eventually ceases, the plates could begin to shift in different directions. Only time will tell whether the Red Sea is an ocean in embryo.

Photographed from the orbiting Gemini XII capsule in 1966, the Red Sea displays a symmetry that points to the time when it was a mere crack between Africa and Saudi Arabia. If the separation continues, the sea may become an ocean. The Red Sea lies at the junction of three tectonic plates (below). As the plates pull apart, new oceanic crust is created. Scientists disagree on when the breakup began; it may have started 50 million years ago.

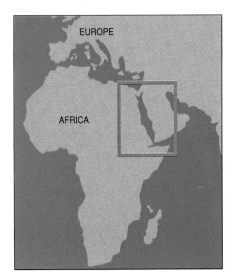

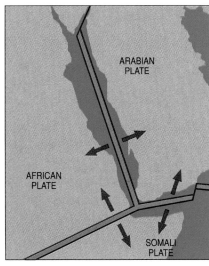

More recently, geologists have gathered a substantial body of other scientific evidence bearing out this theory of plate tectonics. When Vine and Matthews formulated their theory, they based their main argument on information gleaned from investigations of the magnetic properties of the rock composing the ocean floors. It had been known since the turn of the century that many rock formations on land contained tiny natural compasses in the form of small bits of the mineral magnetite; these were aligned with respect to the Earth's north pole. It was also known that on rare occasions, these particles were oriented in the opposite direction, toward the south pole, a fact that had led researchers to conclude that the magnetic field of the Earth itself had flipped at least once in the planet's history.

Vine and Matthews extended this logic to an analysis of the ocean basins. They drew on experiments in which ships had made passes over sections of the ocean floor towing magnetometers, simple devices that measure minute local variations in the intensity of the Earth's natural magnetic field, the lines of magnetic force than run between the North and South Poles. The magnetometer charts revealed that the field strength along the sea floor fluctuated in a distinctive pattern. On the charts the fluctuations appeared as alternating dark and light bars that varied in thickness, like zebra stripes—some more than 20 miles wide.

In an inspired moment, the two researchers realized that the alternating stripes might represent not dips and surges in field intensity, but total shifts in magnetic orientation. They decided that the Earth's magnetic field must have flip-flopped not just once but many times, and that the record of those reverses had been preserved in the rock of the sea floor. Each time the polarity had shifted, it was recorded for posterity; the welling up of magma at the mid-oceanic ridge, when cooled, permanently encoded the polarity of the time. As the sea floor spread away from the ridge, roughly half the newly magnetized material moved to one side and half to the other. Like a non-stop tape recording, the ocean floor has preserved a precise record of polarity shifts throughout its history. And since the date of pole reversals have been calculated approximately, the magnetic stripes of the spreading ocean floor document not only the floor's age, but also the rate at which it has spread. All scientists have to do is play back the recording.

Vine and Matthews elaborated their idea in 1963 and were greeted with skepticism, but corroborating data from the mid-oceanic ridges soon confirmed their notion because the banding patterns found on one side of the ridge neatly mirrored those on the other. Today, geologists know that the poles have changed places at least 300 times in 170 million years, although why remains a puzzle.

SAMPLES FROM THE DEEP

Further clues concerning the origins of the ocean basins come from the rocks of which they are composed. Adapting the technology used by oil companies to drill wells on the continental shelves, scientists have succeeded in the remarkable task of bringing up core samples from the sea floor. Commonly several thousand feet in length, these cylindrical samples preserve the deposition patterns of the sea floor, so that scientists can read the history of the basins from them much as they divine a tree's history from its growth rings.

The first deep ocean drilling project—the Mohole Project—sponsored in 1957 by the National Science Foundation, called on specialists from assorted disciplines

A MAGNETIC TAPE RECORDER

As magma wells up from the Earth's mantle at a divergent plate boundary and forms oceanic crust, magnetic particles in the newly created rock are aligned with the Earth's prevailing magnetic field. The ocean crust on both sides of the boundary move away from its birthing location (1), carrying with it a permanent magnetic record encoded in the rocks. Ocean crust formed when the Earth's magnetic field was lined up with the north pole will contain rocks with magnetic particles pointing north. Ocean crust that solidified when the polarity flip-flopped to the south pole bears rocks that "point" in the opposite direction (2). The stripes are symmetrical, indicating that each side of the ocean is a mirror of the other, compelling proof that oceans are created at divergent plate boundaries and then spread apart.

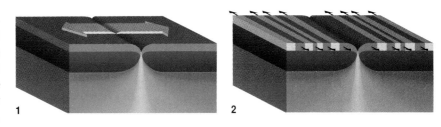

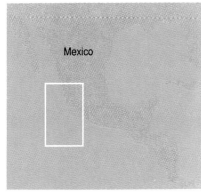

A chart of magnetometer readings taken in the Pacific Ocean shows a zebra-like symmetrical pattern of variations centering on the East Pacific Rise. The beige bands record reversals in the polarity of the Earth's magnetic field. That polarity has switched from the north pole to the south pole hundreds of times throughout Earth's history. The colored bands indicate normal polarity.

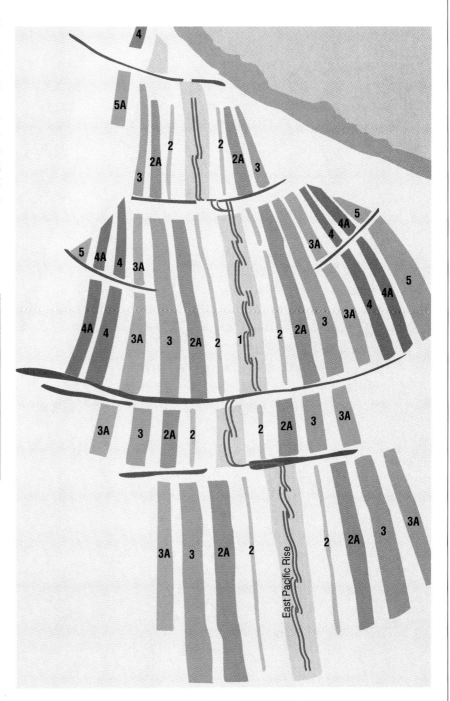

101

all over the world. Their objective was to drill through the Mohorovičic discontinuity, the boundary between the Earth's crust and mantle, which averages 15,000 to 20,000 feet thick under the oceans. Together, oilmen, naval architects, mining engineers and oceanographers pondered the thorny problems involved in positioning a ship in thousands of feet of water and threading a drill into the hard rock of the ocean basins. To succeed, a ship would have to remain virtually stationary for days or weeks at a time while a segmented length of drill pipe more than two miles long carried a bit to the depths. If the ship moved appreciably, the stresses on the pipe—already enormous just from the tension produced by its own weight—would be so great that the pipe would snap. The task has been compared to drilling a hole in a New York sidewalk with a strand of spaghetti suspended from the top of the Empire State Building.

The method designed by the project team was called dynamic positioning, and involved setting up buoys in a circle around the drill ship then monitoring the ship's position in relation to them by sonar. (Later, to ensure that the beacons did not move, more refined drill ships began dropping sound-emitting devices called transponders to the ocean floor.) Four 200-horsepower diesel engines with 16-foot-long shafts and 4-foot-diameter propellers kept the ship centered. The drill pipe itself was designed in sections to stand up to the strain. From top to bottom, the steel casing pipe tapered, with the sections of greatest strength nearest the surface. Heavy collars positioned just above the diamond drill bit helped keep the connected pipe sections—called the drill string—relatively straight. A trumpet-shaped guide shoe that opened downward from the drill-turning rotary table on the ship prevented the pipe from bending too far. And to reduce the stress at the rim of the hole on the ocean floor, a 30-foot-long flexible casing was attached to a landing base. In 1961 tests using a refitted shallow water drilling ship—an ungainly craft with a derrick sprouting from its deck like a futuristic mainmast—a team of scientists from the Mohole Project successfully drilled into the ocean floor to a depth of 12,000 feet, proving the system eminently workable.

Today, an international team of researchers, sponsored by a consortium of institutions and by government agencies called the Joint Oceanographic Institutions for Deep Earth Sampling (JOIDES), is carrying on where Mohole and its successor, the Deep Sea Drilling Project (DSDP), left off. Since 1985, the sophisticated *JOIDES Resolution*, drillship of the Ocean Drilling Program, has pulled up samples from every ocean basin.

On site, the crew puts in 24-hour days as the drill cuts through thousands of feet of basement rock and overlying sediments. The *Resolution*'s mighty dynamic-positioning system keeps the ship directly over the drill hole; the string can continue drilling in waves up to 15 feet high and in water as deep as 27,000 feet. Twelve directional thrusters, along with two fixed propulsion units that deliver 22,600 pounds of thrust apiece, administer correctional shoves. The main props and thrusters are controlled by a computer, which maintains the ship's position by keeping tabs on a sonar beacon that has been deployed ahead of time to the sea floor. In rough seas, the lurching of the vessel is counteracted by pistons that function as a pneumatic spring. The heave compensator, located in the derrick on board the ship, helps maintain constant weight on the drill bit and prevents overloading the drilling assembly. If the ship rocks more than 7°, drilling is halted.

DRILLING CORE SAMPLES

While sonar has stripped away the water and revealed the ocean floor in all its awesome majesty, cylindrical samples of rock and sediment extracted from beneath the oceans have recently given scientists tangible evidence of the fundamental mechanisms that have shaped the ocean floor. Currently, the Ocean Drilling Program is in the process of taking core samples from all of the world's oceans. Since 1987 ODP's drill ship, the *JOIDES Resolution*, has drilled samples from more than 200 sites, in locations as diverse as offshore Antarctica and Baffin Bay.

Once a 30-foot-long core is brought aboard, the crew notes the sample's original location on the sea floor, codes it to distinguish top from bottom and slices it lengthwise. One half is stored for the drilling program's archives. The other section is used by scientists. Paleontologists examine fossils to determine the age of the oldest material and magnetometers are used to read the record of the Earth's magnetic field changes; chemical properties are also studied.

Once a core is extracted—a process that will be repeated many times as the team drills deeper into the ocean floor—scientists lower instruments into the drill hole. In a process called downhole logging, they glean further information by using the instruments to record physical and chemical properties of the surrounding rocks.

A converted oil-drilling ship, the 470-foot-long *JOIDES Resolution* contains seven stories of laboratories where core samples are analyzed.

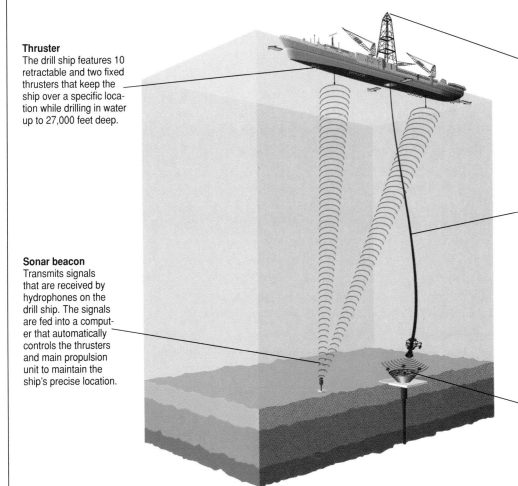

Thruster
The drill ship features 10 retractable and two fixed thrusters that keep the ship over a specific location while drilling in water up to 27,000 feet deep.

Sonar beacon
Transmits signals that are received by hydrophones on the drill ship. The signals are fed into a computer that automatically controls the thrusters and main propulsion unit to maintain the ship's precise location.

Derrick
A 202-foot-tall structure used to raise and lower the drill pipe.

Drill string
Up to 30,000 feet of drill pipe can be screwed together to form what is called a drill string. The cold water of the deep ocean can cause the metal drill string to contract and shrink by three feet for every 14,000 feet of pipe.

Reentry cone
A cone-like device that helps guide the drill string for reentry into a drill hole. For boring directly into hard rock at the sea floor, the assembly is gimballed to compensate for unevenness. Drill operators use a television camera or sonar tool to guide it back into the cone.

The drill string feeds down through the derrick on deck, travels through open water, then passes into an assembly on the sea floor. (Each section of drill pipe, roughly 30 feet long and two-and-a-half inches wide, is threaded to attach to the next section). An engine on the surface turns the drill string with up to 41,000 foot-pounds of torque, and below the four cone-shaped tungsten-carbide drill bits cut into the rock. Sea water is continually pumped down the drill pipe to remove cuttings and cool the bit. As the drill bit eats into the rock, a cylindrical core of undisturbed rock slides through the mouth of the bit into an inner segment of pipe, which researchers periodically retrieve by means of a winch-powered wire that locks onto the core barrel and hauls it to the surface. Once a core is taken on board, scientists make a careful notation of where it was obtained, cut it into five-foot-long sections marked to indicate top and bottom, then split the samples lengthwise. Half of each section goes into the Ocean Drilling Project archives for further reference, the other half is analyzed and tested.

A typical deep-sea cored section might consist of three layers: a topmost layer of sediments several hundred feet thick; a jumbled layer of sediments and basalt that have been slightly altered chemically due to the pressure of the thick sediments above and the circulation of hydrothermally driven fluids; and a solidified base of gabbro, a black, coarse-grained rock, three to four miles thick.

Core samples gathered by the *Resolution* and its workhorse predecessor, the *Glomar Challenger*, have opened a window to the past. From distributions of fossilized flora and fauna in the cores, researchers have divined much about the early climate and landscape of the Earth. A collection of fossil sea creatures unearthed from cores drilled into sediments atop a mountain range may be readily compared with similar fossils taken from other parts of the oceans or on land and their probable time of deposition estimated. Then it is possible to state with some certainty when the mountains themselves lay under water. By examining the physical characteristics of various fossils found in the same layer, or stratum, paleontologists also can tease out information about the environment in which the creatures lived.

They also have learned key facts concerning the nature of the oceanic crust, at the mid-oceanic ridges, along subduction zones and in the abyssal plains. Too, samples have helped establish the age of the sea floor; the oldest chunk of sea floor hauled up dates to 220 million years ago. It came from off the shore of northwestern Australia and dates back to a time when the continents were all joined together in the supercontinent Pangaea.

Scientists arrive at such figures by subjecting samples to radioactive dating, the only means for determining absolutely the age of rocks. Most rocks contain small amounts of radioactive elements. These elements are deemed unstable, because over time they naturally transform, or decay, into other, simpler elements. Certain stable elements, like carbon, also exist in unstable form, possessing in their nuclei more neutrons, or neutrally charged particles, than normal. Essentially, decay involves the steady loss of particles from the nucleus of an atom. So predictable is the decay of a large assemblage of nuclei that each radioactive element or isotope will lose half its given mass within a calculable period of time—its half-life. The half-life of the metallic element rubidium is 500 billion years, which means that 50 percent of a given amount of the radioactive element rubidium will decay into a simpler element, strontium, in that time. The half-life of potassium, another

GUIDANCE FROM ABOVE

Determining the exact position of an ocean-borne craft has always posed a challenge, even to the most meticulous mariner. Such specific knowledge is especially invaluable when drilling core samples or mapping the ocean floor; without an accurate fix, the location of a core sample or a submarine mountain could never be determined precisely.

To pinpoint their locations, today's navigators can consult a network of satellites known as the Navstar Global Positioning System (GPS) orbiting the Earth at a height of 10,900 miles. The orbital pattern of GPS is designed to place at least three satellites in view from anywhere on Earth at any one time. During its twice-daily orbit, each satellite continuously transmits signals to the ground via radio waves. Encoded in each signal is the time according to an onboard atomic clock, which is accurate to within one second in 30,000 years.

GPS receivers—some small enough to fit into a pocket—can pick up these signals and compute position. Synchronized to the satellites' clocks, the computerized receiver can calculate the time it takes for a signal to reach the ship. Since the speed of light is known (186,282 miles per second) as well as the signal's travel time, the distance from ship to satellite can be determined. By knowing its distance from three satellites, the receiver can rapidly deduce its position in two dimensions, longitude and latitude, accurate to within 50 feet or less. The receiver uses a basic geometric principle known as triangulation; simply put, this means that only one point on a plane can be a precise distance from three points (*illustration at right*). By 1993, when the U.S. Department of Defense, which operates GPS, has placed a complete system of 24 satellites in orbit, GPS users can consult a fourth satellite, if necessary, to determine their altitude on storm-tossed seas.

THE GLOBAL POSITIONING SYSTEM

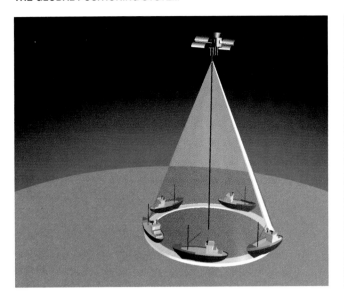

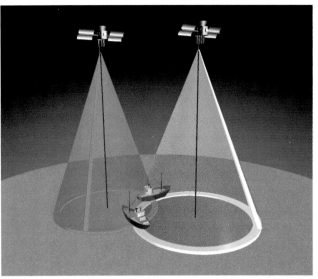

1. Circling in on the position
By measuring the time it takes for a signal to travel from a satellite to a ship, the computer in a GPS receiver deduces that the ship must lie on a circle equidistant to the satellite.

2. Narrowing the choices
Repeating Step 1 but adding a second satellite creates a second circle of possible locations. To be positioned somewhere on two distinct circles means that the two circles must intersect. There are only two places where this can occur. The ship, therefore, must be at one of these two points.

3. Closing the ring
A reading from a third satellite will give the receiver yet another circle on which the ship must lie. However, the ship can only lie on the third circle where it intersects the other two. There is only one place where this can occur—one of the two intersections previously determined. The ship must be where all the circles intersect, a coordinate deduced instantaneously by the receiver.

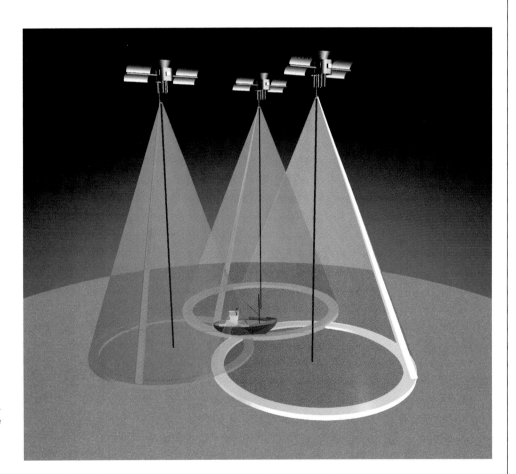

SEARCHING FOR OIL BELOW THE SEA FLOOR

To detect reservoirs of oil trapped under the ocean floor, scientists carry out what is known as a seismic survey. Sound-producing devices are trailed behind a survey ship. On command, they release blasts of air that bounce off the ocean floor and the layers of rock underneath it. The rebounding waves are picked up by ship-towed cables, which contain sensitive listening devices called hydrophones.

The arrival time of the reflection from the subsurface rock formation indicates the depth of the layer. As the ship sails back and forth over a region of the ocean, a computer builds up a series of cross sections. If needed, a three-dimensional map can be created to help locate geological structures that might contain oil or natural gas.

Ultimately, the only way to find out exactly what lies under the ocean floor is to drill an exploratory well. But such an operation is expensive; some offshore drilling units cost a billion dollars to build and more than a quarter of a million dollars a day to operate. Oil companies rely heavily on seismic data to narrow their options.

Hydrophones
Convert the sound energy produced by the reflected sound waves into electrical pulses that are recorded on the survey ship by tape recorders. Later, the data is processed and enhanced by computers.

Air guns
Release sudden bursts of compressed air to generate sound waves that reflect off the layers of rock beneath the ocean floor. Unlike dynamite, which was previously used, geophones do not damage marine life.

Subsurface strata
Underneath the ocean floor the rocks lie in layers, one on top of the other, like the layers of a cake. Laid down originally as sediment and then compressed into rock, the layers are progressively older the deeper they lie.

READING THE CHART

A seismic reflection profile depicts the geological structure under the floor of the North Sea. Scientists use such graphs to look for fault zones (yellow line) that may trap hydrocarbon deposits. Oil and natural gas often move upward, toward an area of lower pressure. Fault zones provide physical barriers that trap that migration.

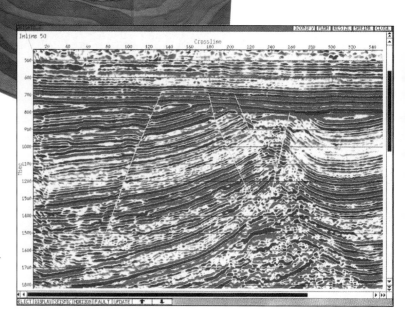

element that is commonly used to date rocks, is 1.28 billion years, after which time half of the mass of the potassium will have turned into the element argon.

By examining the amount of radioactive material in a given rock, scientists can project backward to the time of its formation. Having done this with cores taken from the sea floor, they have confirmed that even the oldest ocean basins are only about one-twentieth as old as the most ancient portions of the continents.

HARVESTING THE WEALTH

Apart from its purely scientific interest, the exploration of the sea floor has another compelling justification: an economic one. Tremendous reserves of oil and natural gas lie untapped beneath the continental shelves and the deep ocean basins. In addition, dozens of other valuable commodities sit locked up in sea floor sediments and basement rocks, some of which may be minable in the near future.

To the industrial world, oil is the premier treasure held by the oceans. As with continental deposits, the petroleum beneath the seas began life as organic matter millions of years ago. Although the subject of petroleum's genesis has been much investigated, geologists cannot yet trace the trail from fern to furnace, as it were, in detail. However, they have outlined the basic steps necessary to the creation of both oil and the natural gas that is so often formed in connection with it.

Millions of years ago, a rain of dead aquatic plants, pollen, spores, skeletons of microscopic water creatures, and other organic material washed in by rivers and streams fell to the bottom of shallow seas, including the fledgling Atlantic. After filling the bottoms of these basins, the material was buried suddenly by a layer of sediment, perhaps in a mud slide or after a tempestuous rainstorm. Once blanketed, the organic ooze did not decay in the normal fashion, since there was very little oxygen to support the aerobic bacteria that normally speed the process.

This series of events may have been repeated numerous times in the history of a given body of water, so that eventually its bottom would be lined with sandwiched organic ooze and sediment. Over time, the weight of the layers would be sufficient to generate enough heat and pressure to transform the loosely packed sediments into stone.

At this point, scientists say, a carefully controlled cooking commenced. To be turned into crude oil, the layers of ooze had to be subjected to pressure and temperatures hovering around 250° F. for hundreds of thousands of years. The longer the cooking went on, the clearer and thinner the oil became. Some of it eventually turned into natural gas.

Left to its own devices, oil rises, sometimes bubbling to the surface in the form of asphaltum, or pitch, as it does widely throughout the Middle East. Ancient Semitic peoples sought out this sticky substance for assorted uses. But for petroleum to gather in sizable quantities, its migration toward the surface must be blocked, or, in the technical parlance, trapped. A trap might be a heavily folded section of the Earth's crust that does not permit the oil to complete its upward progress. Features called salt domes serve the same purpose. They are essentially huge bubbles of salt that have pushed up through overlying sediments; oil often is found around their crowns. Fault zones also serve as traps, locking the oil under layers of impermeable rock. Oil migrates by passing through the tiny holes in rocks called pores, which are not much larger in diameter than a human hair. Petroleum is

Mobile oil rigs like this one in the North Sea are capable of being moved from one drill site to another. Some rest directly on the ocean floor; others float, or are partially submerged to maintain their position. Special burners flare gas harmlessly during a test of the fluids that lie trapped in the reservoir. The first offshore well in the United States was drilled off California at the turn of the 20th Century.

Manganese nodules, metal-rich lumps that form much like pearls in oysters, are strewn like cobblestones over vast areas of the ocean floor, often at a depth of two to four miles. Dissolved minerals in the deep ocean precipitate out of the water and accrete around a nucleus—often a rock fragment or piece of organic debris. Over an incredible period—nodules grow at the rate of one millimeter every million years—individual atoms of manganese and other minerals form thin layers around the nucleus. Various ideas have been devised for mining the nodules, including sucking them from their resting place with a gigantic vacuum-cleaner-like apparatus.

held like water in a sponge rather than like water in a reservoir. Geologists carry out magnetic and gravity field surveys and seismic testing to locate traps. Where there are sedimentary deposits, likely repositories for petroleum, the magnetic field dips, and magnetometers can spot this fluctuation. Similarly, gravimeters, instruments that measure perturbations in the Earth's gravitational field, can pinpoint promising sedimentary formations, since they are less dense than surrounding rock and thus exert less gravity. Seismic surveys analyze the ways in which sound waves move through oceanic rock and produce maps that appear as slices of the Earth. These, too, reveal structures that may trap oil.

Once these steps have yielded a subsea target, wells are drilled. Over the years, engineers have developed two main methods of drilling for oil in the ocean, using rigs that are either floating or partially submerged, or standing on an apron positioned on the sea floor. Floating rigs may sit aboard ships or atop large underwater buoyancy chambers. Far more prevalent are bottom-supported units, which stand on piers that can be retracted so that the rig can be towed from port to sea and back. These self-contained industrial complexes may house up to 300 workers, miles of steel and concrete pipe and assorted other equipment. Forty wellheads may be tapped at a time from one of these rigs. A $1-billion platform probably produces a billion barrels of oil in its lifetime.

For safety's sake, platforms must be built above the level of storm surges, and must be anchored firmly to the sea floor against the fury of the open seas. Despite the precautions, rigs have capsized, killing whole crews. The greatest hazard is a blowout. Thankfully rare, blowouts occur when the oil flowing out of a tapped reservoir, which lets off pressure something like a punctured tire, gushes out so rapidly that it overwhelms the blowout preventer stack, basically a heavy-duty valve at the wellhead that allows drillers to adjust the pressure of the flow. Blowouts can destroy a rig and cause devastating fires, not to mention the environmental devastation caused by spewed crude.

The latest, experimental rigs actually sit on the sea floor, like aquatic versions of a space station. Technicians go below in sub-like crafts or hard suits to monitor well activity, and oil flows to the surface through flexible lines. Such equipment may one day render today's towering platforms obsolete and open the way to recovering oil from even deeper parts of the ocean.

Several other valuable resources abound on the floor of the sea, including strategic and precious minerals whose terrestrial sources are dwindling. Lead, copper, zinc, gold and silver deposits already have been found. Tin has long been mined on the shallow shelf off Thailand's coast, coal on the shelf off Nova Scotia. In some places, sand and gravel for construction are dredged from offshore pits. Geologists estimate that billions of dollars worth of minerals concentrate on the bottom of the Red Sea alone.

Underneath the Red Sea, hot, briny water—stoked by the fire within the mantle—dissolves minerals from the rocks. Expelled from cracks in the sea floor, the rich stew meets the cool water of the sea and, in time, metals such as copper, zinc and silver drizzle out, forming ore deposits on the sea floor. Similar vents, called black smokers, are located along the East Pacific Rise, and they too may produce many valuable byproducts.

Another haul can be found in all the world's oceans in the form of nodules of manganese, a metal much prized as a steel alloy. Manganese nodules, some as large as cannonballs, literally pave portions of the sea floor. Samples were first pulled up during soundings by the 19th-Century H.M.S. *Challenger* expedition, but scientists of the day mistook them for meteorites. Not until the present century did scientists realize that these lumps were rich in manganese and also were sprinkled with valuable metals such as nickel, copper and cobalt. Researchers now know that the nodules form around small bits of material, such as shark's teeth, fragments of bone or tiny pellets of naturally occurring glass. Over millions of years, minute layers of minerals precipitate out of the water and accrete around the core, like the nacreous layers of a pearl.

In recent years, an ambitious scheme to gather manganese nodules has captured the imagination of many mining engineers. To haul the nodules out of the three-to-four miles of water in which they customarily sit, engineers have suggested everything from simple scoops lowered by cable to oversized vacuum cleaners and robots with video cameras for eyes. But such economic ventures might exact unacceptable ecological costs. Tiny microscopic organisms make their homes on the nodules and, for all anyone knows, these small creatures might play a vital role in maintaining the overall biological balance of the oceans—a balance upon which all life on the planet ultimately depends.

VOYAGING TO THE BOTTOM OF THE SEA

T hree hundred-and-fifty miles off the coast of Newfoundland, and nearly two-and-a-half miles down, a tiny blunt-nosed vessel glides slowly forward, its floodlights bathing the underwater darkness in a yellow-green iodide glow. Three mariners—a pilot and two scientists—huddle in the cramped spherical passenger compartment surrounded by control panels, navigation instruments, cameras and scientific gear. Each man peers through a thick plexiglass viewing port, though their visibility is limited. A constant swirl of minute particles and marine organisms—deep-sea divers call it "snow"—restricts the view to perhaps 30 yards.

There are other difficulties. The sonar tracking device that normally pinpoints the sub's position has cut out; without its telltale "pings" the pilot can only guess at his whereabouts. Now another problem develops. Water has begun seeping into the craft's battery pack, threatening to short-circuit the main power supply. A few minutes more, and the mission will have to be scrubbed.

The pilot veers south, risking a final swing across the vacant mud expanse of ocean bottom. All at once, the terrain angles upward, cresting in a sudden berm of silt and heaped boulders. And just beyond, reaching up into the murkiness, looms an immense black steel slab: the hull of a giant ship. Rust spills down the hull plates, obliterating the vessel's name. But there is no mistaking her identity. This is the *Titanic*, the most talked about and written about ocean liner in history—and the object of the little submersible's quest.

It took the very latest tools and techniques of underwater exploration to enable a previous expedition, in the summer of 1985, to pinpoint the *Titanic*'s location on the ocean floor. Now, in July of 1986, Robert Ballard of Massachusetts' Woods Hole Oceanographic Institution—leader of the group that made the initial discovery—has gone down himself for a closer look. His present craft is the three-man submersible *Alvin*, one of several underwater vessels operated by Woods

Her bow covered with long tears of rust, the Titanic *lies submerged yards deep in ocean floor mud. The remotely operated vehicle* Jason Jr.—*headlight ablaze*—*floats at the top right, tethered to the submersible craft* Alvin. *The liner was discovered in 12,500 feet of water in the North Atlantic in 1985.*

Hole scientists. With her pressure-proof spherical bow chamber of two-inch-thick titanium, *Alvin* can dive to 13,000 feet—just far enough to survey the *Titanic*.

When the ship sank in 1912, few dreamt that she would ever be seen again. Now, with the help of late-20th-Century technology, subsurface mariners have not only found her, they have descended to see her firsthand. At one point during the 1986 expedition, *Alvin* even landed on the *Titanic*'s Boat Deck and sent a robot deep inside the wreck to probe what ravages 74 years on the ocean floor had wrought on her once-opulent interior.

Today's underwater explorers can call upon a multitude of diving systems, all custom-tailored to various depths and purposes. A fleet of underwater robots is used for everything from mapping the ocean bottom, to retrieving scientific specimens, surveying shipwrecks and inspecting crab pots for fishermen. Workers in deep diving suits that maintain sea-level pressure of one atmosphere inspect underwater oil wells at enormous depths. And in shallower waters, divers in wetsuits and scuba gear swim about with porpoise-like ease.

THE HUMAN PRESENCE

The urge to explore the ocean depths has inspired mankind since civilization's earliest days. As far back as 4500 B.C., the rulers of Mesopotamia sent divers to the floor of the Persian Gulf to hunt for ornamental seashells. The Greeks and Phoenicians scoured the Mediterranean for sponges and for coral, which they traded for pearls brought up by the divers of India and China. Their methods were simple and their time on the bottom short. The early divers would take a gulp of air, clutch a rock in each hand to weigh themselves down, and jump in. For more extended periods underwater, the air had to be brought down to the diver. One obvious method was to use a breathing tube—a reed or hollow bone—that acted as a prototype snorkel. The divers of Sparta most likely employed a device of this sort when, in 425 B.C., they swam through a blockade of Athenian ships to bring supplies to their beleaguered comrades. The ancients also supplied themselves with air by using large inverted buckets. As long as the bucket was held upside down, the pressure of the surrounding water kept the air trapped within and available to any diver in need of a quick breath.

The inverted bucket functioned, in essence, as a diving bell—a device that assumed major importance in later centuries. Enlarged and sometimes equipped with viewing ports, the bells became underwater chambers in which one or more divers could work on the bottom more or less at will. By the 17th Century A.D., the bells had become standard equipment for salvaging wrecks and other underwater operations. During the middle of the century, a group of salvagers in Sweden used a primitive diving bell to bring up more than 50 bronze cannon from the wreck of the *Vasa*, which sank in Stockholm harbor in 1628.

There were problems, to be sure. The bells were unwieldy, and they confined a diver's explorations to a limited radius. Even worse, the air inside them would soon grow stale from the exhaled carbon dioxide. Overstaying meant suffocation. Various schemes were employed to supply the bells with fresh air. One technique was to pump in the air through a hose rigged to a large bellows on the surface—a method suggested in 1689 by French physicist Denis Papin.

Papin's system worked well in depths up to 70 feet, but beyond that it failed.

A DESCENT TO THE ABYSS

For several thousand years, humans were able to explore but a fraction of the ocean's domain. When a person could rely only on a lungfull of air or a breathing tube, much remained out of bounds in a realm often several miles deep. And the problem of darkness and ever-increasing pressure made the oceans as inhospitable as outer space. But with the invention in the last 150 years of such craft as submersibles, bathyscaphes and submarines, which allowed people to take their normal air-endowed environment with them, a new world gradually opened up. Now, no corner of the ocean lies beyond reach.

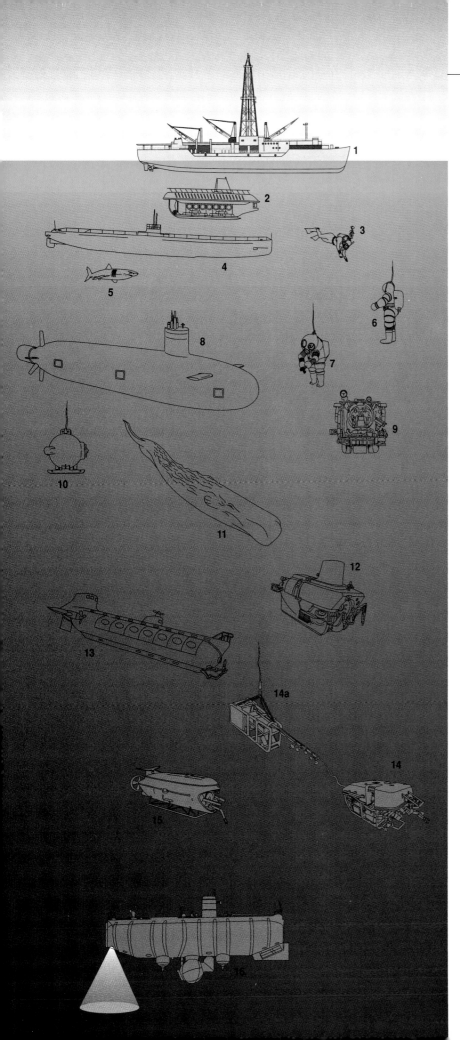

1 **JOIDES RESOLUTION**
470-foot-long ship used to drill the ocean floor for core samples; can extract cores in water as deep as 27,000 feet

2 **ATLANTIS SUBMARINE II**
28-passenger tourist submarine; can dive to depth of 150 feet

3 **SCUBA DIVER**
Co-invented in 1943 by Jacques-Yves Cousteau and Emile Gagnan, the self-contained underwater breathing apparatus carries a supply of compressed air. In 1968 two divers descended to a record-setting 437 feet off Freeport, Grand Bahama, with scuba; most divers stay within 100 feet of the surface.

4 **WORLD WAR II SUBMARINE**
Most traveled close to the ocean's surface, but could descend to 400 feet if necessary

5 **GREAT WHITE SHARK**
Frequents the sunlit surface region of the ocean but can dive to 1,000 feet

6 **NEWTSUIT**
Equipped with optional thrusters, this suit—rated to 1,000 feet—combines both mobility and dexterity, allowing a diver to remain at sea-level pressure: 14.7 pounds per square inch (also known as one atmosphere)

7 **JIM SUIT**
A diver used a one-atmosphere Jim suit in 1976 to recover a TV cable 1,440 feet down off the coast of Spain; maximum operating depth: 2,000 feet

8 **SOVIET AKULA-CLASS NUCLEAR SUBMARINE**
Can remain submerged for weeks at a time, relying on its nuclear powerplant; estimates vary on its maximum operating depth; some military analysts say it may be as much as 2,500 feet

9 **JOHNSON-SEA-LINK SUBMERSIBLE**
Manipulator arms allow this manned vessel—rated to 3,000 feet—to perform various functions, including gathering geological and biological samples from the ocean floor

10 **BEEBE AND BARTON BATHYSPHERE**
Naturalist Dr. William Beebe and designer Otis Barton dived to a record-breaking 3,028 feet off Bermuda in 1934

11 **SPERM WHALE**
Individual specimens of the air-breathing mammal have been detected as deep as 8,000 feet

12 **ALVIN**
Veteran of more than 2,000 dives, the submersible has served as the world's most productive underwater scientific research vessel since it first descended below the waves in 1964; can dive to 13,000 feet

13 **ALUMINAUT**
51-foot-long submersible rated to 15,000 feet; retired in 1971

14 **JASON**
Operated remotely from a research vessel on the surface, Jason is equipped with sensitive mechanical hands; rated to 20,000 feet

14a **MEDEA**
Support vehicle for Jason; carries one color and one black and white video camera, as well as a lighting boom with 2,000 watts of incandescent lights

15 **MIR**
The 25-foot-long Russian-built submersible is rated to 20,000 feet; with a three-person crew it can cruise up to 5 knots

16 **TRIESTE BATHYSCAPHE**
Made the deepest dive ever in 1960 to the bottom of the Marianas Trench near Guam—36,000 feet below the surface

BREATHING UNDERWATER

As the system's name implies, scuba—or self-contained underwater breathing apparatus—allows divers to carry their air with them for forays into the aquatic realm. Central to the scuba system are cylinders of air and the regulator. Constructed of either steel or aluminum, the cylinders—also known as tanks—hold compressed air, which allows a volume of air roughly the size of a phone booth to be stored in a tank that can fit on a diver's back. One tank holds enough air for roughly one hour of diving at 60 feet. Inexperienced divers may breathe more rapidly and therefore use up the air more quickly. Other factors, such as a diver's experience and the temperature of the water will also affect how fast the air is used. The deeper a diver goes the shorter the air lasts. At 120 feet, one tank would sustain a diver for only half an hour.

The tanks are attached by a hose to a mouthpiece featuring a device that reduces the pressurized air to ambient pressure. Known as a regulator, the mechanical apparatus is activated automatically, simply by inhaling and exhaling. When a diver breathes in, the inhalation combined with the water pressure pushes a flexible diaphragm inward, which opens the air inlet valve. When a diver breathes out, the exhalation forces the diaphragm back until the next breath, cutting off the air supply. The exhaled air escapes through an outlet valve.

CONTROLLING THE AIR SUPPLY

(1) As a diver inhales, a rubber diaphragm is drawn in and presses on a lever. That, in turn, opens an air inlet valve, permitting compressed air from a tank to enter the mouthpiece. (2) When the diver breathes out, the exhaled air forces the diaphragm out, closing off the air supply and allowing air to escape through an outlet valve into the water.

Wearing scuba equipment, developed in the 1940s, even amateur divers have access to the underwater world; once they were untethered to an air supply above, divers found they could venture scores of feet below the surface.

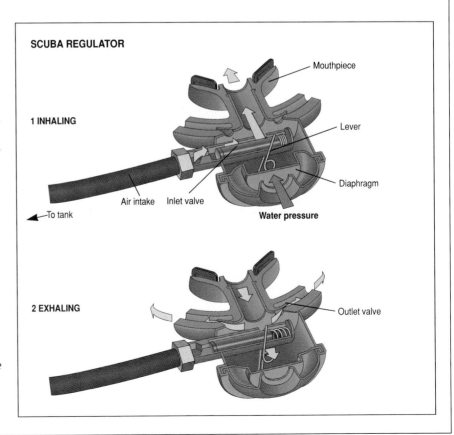

SCUBA REGULATOR

Mouthpiece

1 INHALING

Lever

Air intake   Inlet valve

Diaphragm

To tank

Water pressure

2 EXHALING

Outlet valve

The reason was simple: To prevent a diving bell from flooding, the air confined within it must be kept at a pressure sufficient to equalize the pressure exerted by the water outside. And Papin's bellows were just not powerful enough to accomplish that. Another hundred years would pass before mechanical pumps could deliver the necessary pounds per square inch. But Papin was on to something, for the use of compressed air would eventually become a basic diving technique.

At the surface, a diver breathes in air at atmospheric pressure—14.7 pounds per square inch. But for every foot the diver descends, the press of water upon his chest increases by roughly one-half pound per square inch. Soon the squeeze becomes so great that he cannot expand his lungs. For him to breathe at all, air must be fed to the diver at the same pressure as that of the surrounding water. The deeper he goes, the more pressure he needs.

This basic truth was unknown until comparatively recent times. But by the early 1800s adventurous divers had learned the advantages of a pressurized air supply. And they also began taking advantage of another breakthrough in diving technology: the pressurized diving suit. This began as a kind of miniature, walk-around diving bell, and soon developed into a fully enclosed coverall of watertight canvas with flexible arms and legs, weighted boots, a solid brass helmet and an air hose fitted to an air compressor on the surface. Diving suits greatly expanded the underwater horizon, in both bottom time and accessible depth; but tethered as they were to a surface compressor, they still restricted the diver's scope. Only by carrying an air supply could a diver achieve real freedom.

No one understood this fact more thoroughly than a young French naval officer named Jacques-Yves Cousteau. In the early 1940s, while stationed on the Mediterranean, Cousteau developed a passion for underwater photography. But he wanted to stay down long enough, and move about freely enough, to get good pictures. Cousteau set out to devise a safe, portable air supply. Such systems already existed, albeit in rudimentary form. One basic type worked on the principle of reusing oxygen in a portable tank, and filtering out exhaled carbon dioxide. The prototype had been designed by an Englishman, Henry Fleuss, who in 1868 built what he called a closed-circuit oxygen rebreather for use in coal mines; a chemical scrubber containing caustic soda absorbed the carbon dioxide. The British navy adapted the device for deployment underwater, where it left no telltale bubbles that could be detected by an enemy. Primitive rebreathers had one main drawback, however; they relied on pure oxgen, rather than air, and at pressures below 27 feet, pure oxygen is toxic. Closed-circuit rebreathers, greatly refined, are now standard gear for navy divers worldwide, and they also provide the air supply for everything from submarines to space capsules. But for normal diving, a safer technique clearly was preferable. So Cousteau turned to the best alternative: an open-circuit system using ordinary compressed air. But since air pressure must increase with depth in order for the diver to breathe, a device had to be designed that would adjust itself automatically, delivering precisely the right amount of air as the diver breathed in, and then closing to conserve the supply while the diver exhaled. An engineer friend, Emile Gagnan, created a demand regulator, with a diaphragm that closed and opened a valve only when a diver breathed—and so sparked yet another revolution in diving capability.

When Cousteau tried out the new demand regulator and compressed air backpack, the result surpassed his wildest dreams. "I reached the bottom in a state of transport," he wrote later. "At night I had often had visions of flying by extending my arms as wings. Now I flew without wings." Millions of others since have experienced the same sensation. Cousteau's Aqualung, as he christened it, was the first reliable scuba (for self-contained underwater breathing apparatus). It is used worldwide by scientists and sportsmen, fishermen and navy frogmen, salvage crews and treasure hunters alike.

A BATTLE AGAINST PRESSURE

Once freed from the surface tether, scuba divers descended a hundred feet and more below the surface. But there they encountered a problem that had plagued deep-sea divers before, for the pressures of the ocean—and of the compressed air breathing supply in particular—can pose terrible bodily hazard. The dangers become apparent at depths as shallow as 100 feet. The diver's lips begin to feel numb, the bubbles from his exhaust valve take on a musical sound, a sense of mild euphoria sets in. He is experiencing the first symptoms of nitrogen narcosis—the so-called "rapture of the deep"—which results from breathing nitrogen, the main component of air, under pressure. Nitrogen comprises about 78 percent of air, oxygen another 21 percent; the rest are trace gases such as argon, neon and carbon dioxide. Normally, the nitrogen is inert; but as a diver descends, nitrogen is absorbed into the body, where, in effect, it intoxicates the diver. The deeper he goes, the more intoxicated he becomes. By 180 feet or so, the rapture is so intense that a diver may lose all sense of judgment and concern for self preservation. More than one diver at this depth has been tempted to offer his regulator to a passing fish.

Professional divers regularly go down to more heroic depths in deep-diving suits. To avoid this nitrogen narcosis they simply forgo nitrogen; the air in their surface-fed breathing hose is a gaseous "cocktail" in which the nitrogen has been replaced by one or more other gases. The most widely used mixture is heliox, which consists of helium and oxygen. The helium has certain bizarre side effects, though. Being lighter than nitrogen, it allows the vocal chords to vibrate faster, so that the diver sounds a bit like Donald Duck when he communicates with people on the surface. It also conducts heat away from the body, with potentially chilling effect. And at extreme depths helium can cause neurological damage. For this reason, some mixtures include a small amount of nitrogen in what is known as a trimix—helium, oxygen and nitrogen. The nitrogen counteracts the neurological effects produced by the helium.

At the depth of about 300 feet, yet another peril sets in: oxygen poisoning. At this level, where the ambient pressure reaches 132 pounds per square inch, the lungs absorb even dilute oxygen at a dangerous rate. Physiologists are unsure why breathing oxygen under pressure wreaks havoc with the central nervous system. One theory suggests that it interferes chemically with enzymes used by the tissues for metabolism. To compensate, the gas mixture must be adjusted, with the oxygen reduced to as little as 4 percent—at which concentration the lungs take it in as

A PROBLEM OF PRESSURE

A diver breathing air under pressure absorbs nitrogen into the bloodstream in a dissolved form (top). If the person ascends too rapidly, the release of pressure will cause the nitrogen to form bubbles (bottom)—in much the same way that a shaken soda bottle fizzes when the cap is removed quickly. The result is a painful, possibly fatal disorder called decompression sickness, or the bends. If the diver ascends slowly enough, however, the pressure is released gradually and the nitrogen diffuses naturally out of the body through exhalation with no ill effects.

though breathing air at sea level. In trips to extreme depths, where the diver experiences a constantly shifting spectrum of pressures and absorption rates, the breathing cocktail must be readjusted a number of times by a support crew stationed on the surface as the diver descends.

The most notorious diving syndrome of all is the agonizing condition known as decompression sickness or the bends. Its earliest victims, in the mid-19th Century, were coal miners and bridge builders who worked long shifts under ground. One standard method of laying a bridge foundation was to perform the work inside a caisson—basically a large diving bell fed with compressed air to keep out the water. But upon emerging from the caisson, some workers would be attacked by dizziness, nausea and excruciating pains in muscles and joints. Some were left permanently crippled; others died. Their contorted bodies reminded colleagues of a current fad, in which fashionable ladies affected a slouching posture known as the Grecian Bend: hence the name. But no one knew what caused the condition or how to correct it.

The explanation, discovered in the late 1870s by French physiologist Paul Bert, has to do with another ill effect of breathing under pressure. A certain amount of atmospheric gas is always present in the body, dissolved in the blood and tissues, and as the pressure increases still more becomes absorbed. This is no problem—so long as the pressure is maintained. But if the pressure is suddenly released, as when a diver or a caisson worker ascends too quickly to the surface, the body has no time to void the excess. The dissolved gas, most of it nitrogen, starts bubbling out of the solution. The explosion of nitrogen bubbles clogs small veins and arteries, blocking circulation to one or more parts of the body. The most dangerous area afflicted are the nervous system and the brain.

Bert also suggested the obvious preventative, which is to come up slowly enough for the nitrogen bubbles to remain in solution and leave the body safely through the lungs. Alternatively, a surfacing professional diver can enter an on-site decompression chamber and gradually be brought up to atmospheric breathing conditions. The device will also alleviate symptoms that have already started; the operator simply cranks up the pressure and the victim's bubbles redissolve.

The bends remains a major threat, however, even for dives as shallow as 40 feet. How much nitrogen the body absorbs hinges on how deep the diver goes and how long he stays at any particular depth. The more total pressure a diver is subjected to, the greater the potential hazard and the more time needed to decompress. Carefully devised tables give the proper ascent rates and decompression periods. A one-hour dive at 100 feet, for example, necessitates spending 40 minutes to surface. For a one-hour plunge to 250 feet, a diver has to take more than 6 hours to ascend. Slow decompression is essential even when other gases are substituted for nitrogen. The absorption rates change, but the danger persists.

Because decompression is such a lengthy process, divers make every effort to reduce the need for it. One way is to stay down so briefly that nitrogen absorption is kept to a minimum. The other is to accept the consequences of long-term exposure, remaining at maximum depth until the body has absorbed as much nitrogen as it ever will at that particular depth and pressure. The rest of the dive then becomes all free time. The diver can stay six hours, or six days, and his decompression schedule will be the same.

This technique, called saturation diving, is particularly useful in lengthy commercial operations such as the repair and maintenance of deep-sea oil rigs. If the divers are working at a depth of 600 feet, they stay at that same pressure during their off-duty hours, living in a pressurized chamber aboard ship. A pressurized diving bell ferries them up and down to work. A typical saturation dive might last as long as 20 days, during which the divers remain totally isolated from normal atmospheric life. Then, their diving tour over, they must spend six days decompressing. But they go through the process only once during their 20-day stint. With all its current safeguards, pressurized breathing continues to pose strict limits on the undersea horizon. One possible alternative—liquid breathing—remains in the realm of science fiction although laboratory tests have nudged it closer to reality. As the name suggests, the method proposes temporarily converting humans to aquatic animals. Water—H_2O—contains oxygen, but in relatively small amounts; water at sea level has the same oxygen content as the rarefied air at 70,000 feet. If the oxygen content is increased with the use of pressurized air or an oxygen-rich fluid, however, mammals are capable of extracting more of the life-sustaining substance. Mice have survived in a solution composed of water, compressed oxygen and dissolved salts for up to 18 hours. In experiments a human has "breathed" an oxygenated fluorocarbon liquid in one lung for an hour while breathing air with the other lung and suffered no ill effects. Liquid breathing offers distinct advantages—for one, a continuous supply of oxygen. Also, because the diver would be relying on a liquid, which is not compressible, the possibility exists that he would be able to dive thousands of feet and pop back to the surface without the usual attendant medical syndromes. Still, no way has been uncovered to eliminate the carbon dioxide produced, which is normally dissipated in regular breathing by the air. And a buildup of carbon dioxide would eventually suffocate a diver.

Another alternative to pressurized breathing already exists, however. Given the right equipment, voyaging into the ocean depths may be done entirely at atmospheric pressure. The voyager merely has to take the surface environment down with him. One method in vogue currently is to encase the diver in a hard metal suit that shields him from the pressures of the surrounding ocean. Since his chest is not squeezed by the weight of water overhead, he can breathe at normal pressure. Some of the latest atmospheric diving suits—or ADS, as these systems are acronymically dubbed—are totally independent of the surface, with back-mounted thrusters that can raise them, lower them, or drive them forward at a knot-and-a-half of speed. In short, the diver is sheathed in a body-fitting, walkabout one-man submarine that can take him to the lowermost edges of the continental shelf, as far as 2,000 feet below the surface.

One of the most innovative designs is the flexible NEWTSUIT, developed in the mid-1980s by Canadian designer Phil Nuytten. Built of aluminum, the suit features 20 waterproof rotary joints of Teflon and titanium. Oil serves as the bearing. Each joint contains a free-floating central piston that resists the pressure that would otherwise threaten to seize up the joints. (At 1,000 feet—the maximum rated operating depth of the NEWTSUIT—water pressure presses in at more than 400 pounds per square inch.)

A winch lowers the diver to the prescribed depth; lead weights bolted to the front and back of the suit—adjusted for the weight of the diver—maintain the proper buoyancy. The backpack contains four bottles of oxygen, good for 48 hours in all. Inside the suit, a small fan circulates the air through a chemical scrubber that absorbs the diver's exhaled carbon dioxide. The suit contains its own battery pack, and communication is by a radio-like device called a hydrophone, which sends out high-frequency sonar signals. (Since radio waves do not travel well through water, acoustical waves must be substituted; the conversational effect is no different, however.) An optional thruster pack, which allows the diver to move independently, consists of a 1.5-horsepower motor that drives two variable-pitch propellers.

All atmospheric suits are costly to buy—as much as $400,000 for the NEWTSUIT—and expensive to operate. A single day's dive may run $10,000, including the salaries of a four-man support crew. But compared to the fee for a saturation dive, this figure is bargain basement. A typical saturation dive may require a support crew of 20 to 24 to handle 100 tons of equipment, including the diving bell, air compressors and the decompression chamber. A doctor must be present, in case anyone should develop the bends. Then there are the breathing mixtures, including the rare gas helium. All told, the cost for a diver working a full day at 1,000 feet can easily exceed $100,000.

SUBMERSIBLES TO THE RESCUE

Beyond the brink of the continental shelf, where the ocean plunges thousands of feet, well below the range of even the deepest-diving ADS, another technology must be brought to bear. Here, where the environment is as inhospitable to human life as the near-vacuum of outer space, the submarine and its younger cousin, the manned submersible, come into their own. (The distinction between the two is one of travel: submersibles' journeys are usually vertical, whereas submarines are capable of traveling long distances horizontally underwater.) Even at 13,000 feet below sea level—the range in which *Alvin* explored the *Titanic*—water pressure reaches a rivet-popping 6,000 pounds per square inch. In such places as the Atlantic's Puerto Rico Trough—more than 30,000 feet deep—the water presses every square inch of surface with a force of nearly seven tons.

The design best suited to withstand these pressures is a sphere—the shape of *Alvin*'s crew compartment, and that of every other deep-diving submersible. The first to recognize the shape's use was the zoologist William Beebe who, in the 1930s, had himself lowered by cable inside a heavy steel ball that he called a bathysphere. His farthest descent, with designer Otis Barton, was a then-astonishing 3,028 feet. This was more than five times the depth that any human being had

The flexibility of the NEWTSUIT is demonstrated by a diver turning a valve, while kneeling in an underwater simulation tank. In the past, hardsuits allowed workers to descend well beyond the limits of scuba divers, but permitted little movement. The NEWTSUIT features fluid-filled joints that remain flexible even under 700 pounds of pressure per square inch. Its builders boast that it offers 75 percent of normal mobility. The suit weighs 600 pounds on land, but is weightless in water.

yet ventured into the ocean abyss and returned to tell about it. Still, it paled next to the dive made in 1960, when Frenchman Jacques Piccard and U.S. Navy Lieutenant Don Walsh boarded the bathyscaphe *Trieste* and descended 35,820 feet to the bottom of the Pacific Ocean's Marianas Trench. The vessel featured a six-and-a-half-foot diameter steel sphere with walls six inches thick and exterior tanks filled with gasoline. Lighter than water, the liquid provided buoyancy to help send the craft back up to the surface; disposable iron pellets provided the ballast to sink the craft. The diving time was eight-and-a-half hours, which included a 20-minute stay on the ocean floor. It was the deepest dive ever, to the lowest known spot on Earth. So severe was the pressure and temperature changes that paint was stripped off the hull of the little passenger sphere suspended from the bottom of *Trieste*'s hull.

Bathyscaphes remain the ultimate deep-diving vessels. But they lack mobility; *Trieste* sported propellers near her bow, but battery power limited the craft's range to four miles. And besides, most useful science, and most commercial work as well, is performed at shallower depths. A fleet of manned submersibles thus navigates the broad mid-ocean spectrum between 1,000 and 15,000 feet. These vehicles range from the U.S. Navy's 10-man nuclear-powered research submarine, *NR-1*, which can voyage three weeks along the Mid-Atlantic Ridge without once breaching the surface, down to one-man, self-propelled minisubs.

The versatile, one-man *Deep Rover* is one of many such designs—a five-foot diameter clear plastic globe resting on a square base, resembling the glass globes that, when shaken, produce miniature snowfalls. The five-inch-thick sphere is hinged like a clam shell; the deeper it goes—and *Deep Rover* can safely descend to 3,000 feet—the more the water pressure pushes in on the craft and the tighter the seal. A battery of dials, screens and sensors is close at hand: search light, strobe flasher, radio gear, an acoustic communications rig, a pair of compasses, a color video camera and a sonar screen that reveals the bottom terrain in three-dimensional color. Various dials monitor the equipment that recycles air—the oxygen release and carbon dioxide scrubber. The pilot has battery power for an eight-hour dive, and life support gear that can sustain him for an entire week. Sprouting from the front of the craft is a pair of six-foot manipulator arms that each can heft 200 pounds, but which are so precise that the pilot can use them to sign his name. When sensors at their tips touch an object, they transmit an acoustic signal that varies in pitch with the hardness and texture of the material being touched. Four thrusters move the craft in any direction with astonishing ease. Says designer Graham Hawkes, *Deep Rover* was made "so simple even a scientist can operate it."

Manned submersibles have long been the pioneers of underwater research, giving scientists a sense of firsthand discovery that no videotape or computer readout can ever match. And of all the research vessels none has made so many dives, or brought back so much astonishing new information, as *Alvin*. The first of the modern submersibles, *Alvin* was launched in 1964—a squat, stubby 16-ton, 23-foot-long craft that reminded one witness of a puffed-up blowfish. Few scientists expected much from her; at the time most data was obtained with such techniques as echo sounding, deep trawling and dredging up sediments with rigs mounted on surface vessels. Even the U.S. Navy, *Alvin*'s owner of record, and some of the scientists at Woods Hole who had charge of her operation, were skeptical. But it did not take long for *Alvin* to prove her worth.

WORKHORSE OF THE DEEP

With more than a quarter of a century of service and 2,200 dives in its log, the research vessel *Alvin* is the world's most successful submersible, taking part in geological and biological work throughout the world's oceans. Launched in 1964, the craft was named after its major supporter, Allyn Vine, a scientist at *Alvin*'s home base, the Woods Hole Oceanographic Institution in Massachusetts.

Originally designed to operate down to 6,000 feet, *Alvin* has gone through several complete overhauls; no original parts remain. The craft's present titanium seven-foot sphere can withstand pressure of more than five tons per square inch. In fact, the vessel could venture deeper than its 13,000-foot rating, but in doing so it would eventually sustain a type of metal fatigue known as creep, which would weaken its structure much as repeated aerodynamic stress on an airplane weakens its fuselage.

Titanium sphere
Forty percent lighter than steel, titanium is one of the strongest metals, used on everything from spacecraft to fighter aircraft. *Alvin*'s seven-foot-sphere carries one pilot and two passengers.

Sail
Five-foot-high conning tower used to enter titanium sphere.

Hoisting bitt
A titanium T-bar situated directly over *Alvin*'s center of gravity, used for hoisting *Alvin* on and off its mother ship, *Atlantis II*.

Syntactic foam
Billions of the tiny air-filled glass bubbles, bound togther by an epoxy matrix, provide *Alvin* with buoyancy to keep it suspended in water without rising or sinking.

Thrusters
Four thrusters and two midship props powered by small electric motors can drive *Alvin* up to two knots.

Viewing port (3)
Four-inch diameter windows made of plexiglass.

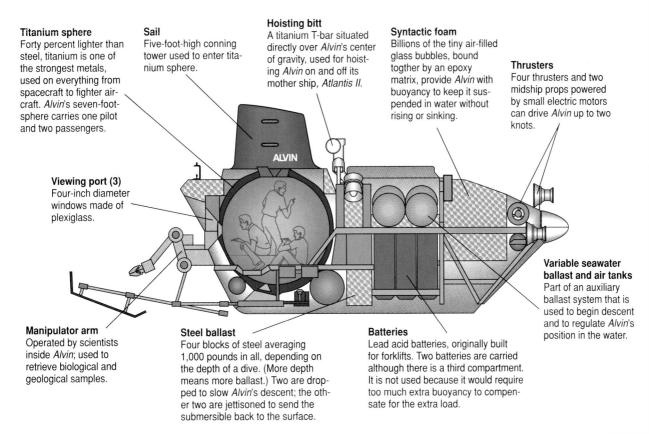

Variable seawater ballast and air tanks
Part of an auxiliary ballast system that is used to begin descent and to regulate *Alvin*'s position in the water.

Manipulator arm
Operated by scientists inside *Alvin*; used to retrieve biological and geological samples.

Steel ballast
Four blocks of steel averaging 1,000 pounds in all, depending on the depth of a dive. (More depth means more ballast.) Two are dropped to slow *Alvin*'s descent; the other two are jettisoned to send the submersible back to the surface.

Batteries
Lead acid batteries, originally built for forklifts. Two batteries are carried although there is a third compartment. It is not used because it would require too much extra buoyancy to compensate for the extra load.

121

She earned her laurels in the most dramatic manner imaginable when two U.S. bombers collided in midair over Palomares, Spain, sending an unarmed H-bomb—hundreds of times more powerful than the atomic bomb that destroyed Hiroshima—into the Mediterranean. *Alvin* was dispatched to find it. The mission took 35 dives and eight weeks and cost the United States $12 million. Rear Admiral William Guest, director of the search, likened the task to finding a .22 caliber bullet in a muddy, water-filled Grand Canyon using only a penlight. But locate it she did, lodged in the mud under 2,310 feet of water. Gingerly steering the sub through the murky waters of the sea floor, *Alvin*'s pilots managed to avoid ensnaring their craft in the bomb's parachute or bumping into the warhead's protective casing. One false nudge could have released clouds of radioactivity or set off the TNT inside the device. Then, with the help of the navy's Cable Controlled Underwater Research Vehicle (CURV), a remotely controlled vehicle that normally retrieved spent torpedoes, the H-bomb was hoisted to the surface.

Alvin moved on to other triumphs. Beginning in 1974, in the three-year Project FAMOUS, she took part in the first manned probes of the Mid-Atlantic Ridge, where sea-floor spreading drives the continents apart. Here she discovered new lava formations, and an exuberance of life at 9,000 feet where hardly any life had been thought to exist. She moved on to the Caribbean's Cayman Trough, descending to 12,000 feet and bringing back a treasure trove of geologic data. Then in 1977, while exploring the Galápagos Rift off Equador, she happened upon clusters of hydrothermal vents—undersea geysers that pour forth superheated water rich in sulphur. Bacteria in creatures surrounding the vents used the sulphur as a substitute for sunlight to synthesize food *(pages 60-64)*.

Alvin's exterior, reinforced with a titanium frame and reconfigured over the years, derives its buoyancy from a substance known as syntactic foam. Millions of air bubbles encased in near-microscopic spheres are held captive in an epoxy matrix. Blocks of the foam, molded into the hull, provide 4,000 pounds of lift. They perform the same function, in effect, as the gasoline-filled hull of a bathyscaphe. Once in the water, *Alvin* floats on the surface like an ordinary boat, but in order to submerge the pilot must decrease her buoyancy by filling her main ballast tanks with seawater. (A variable ballast system also allows *Alvin*'s pilot to adjust the craft's position in the water.) Two other tanks—one aft, the other forward—serve to fine-tune *Alvin*'s trim; by pumping mercury from one to the other, the pilot causes the bow to tilt down, or up, or to ride on an even keel.

A JOURNEY IN *ALVIN*

A typical dive in *Alvin*—to 8,000 feet, say, to pick up rock samples and biological specimens near a hydrothermal vent—might last eight hours. Preparations start well in advance, with an extensive survey of the dive site. First, *Alvin*'s mother ship pinpoints its location within several feet accuracy by means of triangulation, receiving signals from three of the Global Positioning System's network of satellites *(pages 104-105)*. The bottom contours of the ocean are mapped up to two years in advance by cameras and a sonar sled towed beneath the surface. An array of sonar-activated beacons then is deployed along the ocean floor. During the dive, these signals will serve as reference points that allow a computer aboard *Alvin*'s mother ship to track the sub's progress. In fact, because visibility can be limited near the ocean floor, the dive crew on the mother ship has a better picture of *Alvin*'s whereabouts at any particular moment than the sub's own pilot. The surface navigator plots *Alvin*'s course on a bottom chart spread out before him, and calls down any needed changes in heading via an accoustic communications system.

Alvin's present mother craft is the research vessel *Atlantis II*, out of Woods Hole. She is a welcome advance over the sub's first tender, the barge-like catamaran *Lulu*, which was cobbled together from a pair of mothballed Navy pontoons. Now *Lulu* is herself mothballed, and *Alvin* sits cradled on *Atlantis II*'s fantail while her pilot runs through a 14-page pre-dive checklist. Equipment for the day's mission—scoops, nets, specimen boxes and water-sampling bottles—is positioned in the basket mounted on the sub's prow, within easy reach of the manipulator arm. The pilot and two marine scientists enter through *Alvin*'s sail (no one calls it a conning tower), and climb down into the cramped sphere. The hatch is sealed. Space is so tight that neophyte passengers are given a pre-run 30-minute tryout with the hatch closed to weed out the claustrophobic. At a signal from the dive's surface controller, an A-frame crane lifts *Alvin* off the fantail and into the water. The pilot floods the main ballast tanks and the dive begins.

The little sub freefalls gently toward the bottom at 100 feet per minute. If currents are strong in the area, *Alvin* might be dropped a mile or more upstream from

KEEPING IN TOUCH

As Alvin *maneuvers on the ocean floor, its position is monitored by a support ship,* Atlantis II, *which can triangulate the submersible's location by using three transponders that are dropped before the dive begins.* Alvin *carries its own transponder; when it sends out a sonar signal, each of the stationary transponders replies with its own unique signal. The submersible's pilot communicates with* Atlantis II *by sending acoustic signals.*

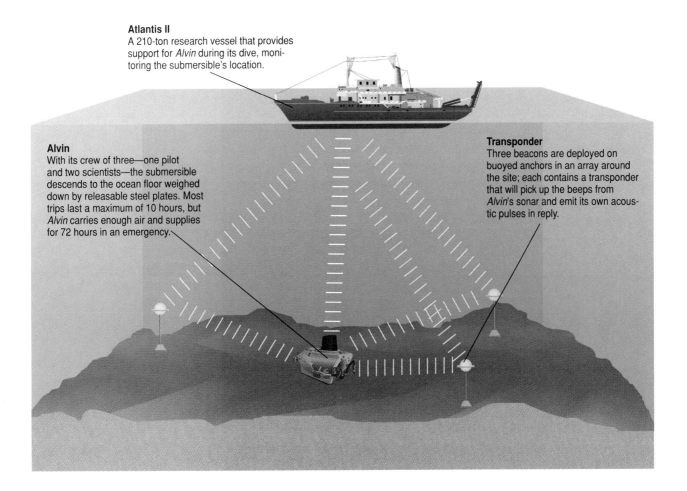

Atlantis II
A 210-ton research vessel that provides support for *Alvin* during its dive, monitoring the submersible's location.

Alvin
With its crew of three—one pilot and two scientists—the submersible descends to the ocean floor weighed down by releasable steel plates. Most trips last a maximum of 10 hours, but *Alvin* carries enough air and supplies for 72 hours in an emergency.

Transponder
Three beacons are deployed on buoyed anchors in an array around the site; each contains a transponder that will pick up the beeps from *Alvin*'s sonar and emit its own acoustic pulses in reply.

BARREL ROLLING WITH THE WHALES

Research submersibles always have transported their crews through the ocean vertically, like underwater elevators. They descended and ascended by using ballast and buoyancy. Having reached a site, these dwarf submarines moved horizontally, but at barely one knot, until engineer Graham Hawkes designed *Deep Flight.* Moonlighting with a group of keen colleagues at his own company, Deep Ocean Engineering, Hawkes swapped ballast for lift and built an experimental winged submersible that can fly through the ocean.

Piloted by one person lying prone in the craft's "people pod," the hydrodynamically shaped sub relies on battery-powered thrusters and the principles of lift to wing its way through water at 12 knots, its maximum speed.

Deep Flight monitors the pathway ahead with an electronically scanning sonar that provides a high resolution image of the coming 300 feet—the image is updated eight times a second. Aside from helping the driver negotiate his watery way, the sonar system can perform search and survey tasks. Locating a downed aircraft on the ocean floor, for example, can be slow and laborious using sonar systems or remotely operated vehicles tethered to a ship. *Deep Flight* operates independently of a mother ship, and can cover approximately 50 square miles in 12 hours—the proposed limit for a single outing based on air supply and operator comfort. Should it break down during a mission, *Deep Flight's* positively buoyant design will usher it automatically back to the surface, its nose pitched upward at 30 degrees.

DEEP FLIGHT

With its two sets of wings, Deep Flight is designed to ascend and descend at 6 knots or 600 feet per minute and plane out into horizontal flight at any depth down to 10,000 feet. The 22-foot-long vessel is scheduled to take its first plunge by Fall 1991.

its ocean floor target to compensate for drift. As the sphere descends, the light soon fades from the three plexiglass viewing ports; the sea is as black as squid's ink. And icy cold: The temperature inside the titanium sphere drops to 55°F, and moisture condenses overhead. (During Robert Ballard's first dive in Alvin, the *Titanic's* future discoverer noticed droplets on the inside of the craft and was convinced that it had started to leak. The pilot assured him that the condensation was, in fact, normal.) The passengers don sweaters. *Alvin* also comes equipped with emergency down sleeping bags. Without them, a crew stranded in an emergency would die of hypothermia before the air supply in the submersible finally gave out.

At 600 feet from the bottom the pilot slows the craft's descent by shedding steel ballast until *Alvin* hangs about a dozen feet off the bottom. Touching bottom would stir up clouds of sediment that would cut visibility. Even so, vision through the viewing ports is 40 yards at best because of lighting limitations. But the scientists are glued to their windows on this watery world. Before them lies an astonishing landscape of frozen vulcanism: great boulders of pillow lava, the diamond-sharp sparkle of obsidian. Ahead there rises a sulfurous yellow chimney that spews out superheated water. Crabs, giant clams and six-foot-long tubeworms proliferate. The pilot works the manipulator arm, plucking loose rock and tubeworms and placing them in the collection basket. If currents on the bottom are stronger than

Alvin's two knot top speed, the pilot might use the craft's manipulator arm to hold fast to a rock or some other convenient tether.

Next *Alvin* is guided into an underwater canyon, an operation of some delicacy. Of all the dangers the sub might encounter—and it has faced many, including an underwater landslide and an attack by an enraged swordfish who jammed its sword into a gap between *Alvin's* passenger sphere and the craft's fiberglass skin—the worst is to become wedged between rocks. Various safety features are designed for a quick escape. The manipulator can be jettisoned and the collection basket shed. One or more battery banks also can be let go. That failing, the passenger sphere can be severed from the remainder of the vehicle by turning a T-bar on the floor of the craft. The sphere, buoyed by its syntactic foam skin, will shoot to the surface. Some have questioned whether the crew would survive such an escape, however. Released from its imprisonment on the ocean floor, *Alvin* might wiggle erratically to the surface, mercilessly rattling crew and racks of equipment. Luckily, no such sudden exit has ever been required.

The normal procedure is to alert the surface controller, who gives clearance to ascend. The pilot then drops a set of 500-pound ballast plates, causing *Alvin* to rise at the same leisurely pace that carried her down. After she breaks the surface, divers from *Atlantis II* secure the ship's crane to the lifting bar welded aft of *Alvin's* sail. Within 15 minutes of surfacing, the craft is back sitting safely on the deck of its mother ship.

ROBOTS OF THE DEEP

For all the hands-on excitement of a voyage into the depths, the newest frontier in subsurface exploration requires no human presence. Much of the scientific data fished up from the bottom—and a growing proportion of the commercial work done there as well—is being handled by underwater robots. These Remotely Operated Vehicles, or ROVs, can be deployed at a fraction of the cost of a manned dive—and at virtually no hazard—to brave fierce crosscurrents and to probe caves, canyons and wrecked ships where no submersible could safely venture. Well over a thousand ROVs are now in use, and they range in size from multi-ton giants that must be launched by cranes, down to compact 40-pound portables not much bigger than a suitcase. And with the continuing improvement in sensing techniques and in microchip circuitry, they can summon up the underwater environment in such vivid detail that it seems almost as good as being there.

The first ROVs were built by the military, for such top-secret tasks as retrieving missiles and parts of sunken combat vessels. One of the earliest was the U.S. Navy's CURV, which swam into prominence during the episode of the lost H-bomb. Since then, other ROVs have surveyed wrecked Russian submarines, swept mines from the Persian Gulf and recovered downed aircraft. Oil companies have become ROV enthusiasts, too; they use robots to cut and weld metal, to drill, rivet and tighten bolts. Other companies are concerned with inspecting and servicing equipment on the ocean floor. AT & T Bell Laboratories have designed two 6,300-pound robots called SCARAB (Submersible Craft for Assisting Repair and Burial), to service undersea transatlantic cables (*pages 90-91*). The multi-million dollar ROVs are linked to a mother ship by a 10,000-foot umbilical cable, which transmits commands to the robot's prehensile claw. In 1985, SCARAB retrieved the flight recorders of an Air India 747, which was blown up by a terrorist bomb over the North Atlantic in June of that year and sank in 6,700 feet of water.

The current trend, though, is toward smaller and cheaper designs. The Phantom series, produced in the U.S. by the expatriate Briton Graham Hawkes, includes models that weigh less than 40 pounds and retail for as little as $16,000—well within the budget of a university oceanography department. The Phantom *DS4*, which sells for $100,000, is typical of today's more upscale ROVs. Compact enough to be launched and controlled from a small motorboat, it is has six electric-powered thrusters, a manipulator arm, optional sonar, and a battery of high-intensity lights and photographic gear that can transmit detailed color images from depths of 1,500 feet and more. Its computerized video camera sends the information to a monitor screen on the surface via fiber-optic cable. Data is encoded as pulses of light beamed through strands of very pure glass. So fine are the fibers that five miles of the hairlike strands could be coiled up in a coffee can. An outer jacket provides strength and protection. At the receiving end, a photodetector senses the pulses and translates them back into electrical signals.

When the operator spots an image he wants to preserve, he touches off a still camera hooked to synchronized strobe lights. The Phantom *DS4* has captured pictures of a volcanic crater 1,000 feet below the surface of the Pacific, and has plunged beneath Antarctica's Ross Sea Ice Shelf to bring back photos of giant sponges and cavorting seals. In supercool Antarctic waters several degrees below freezing, where a human diver in a wet suit can survive only 30 minutes, the Phantom has functioned for more than 15 hours at a stretch.

Advances in mechanical engineering have brought a remarkable agility to the manipulator claws on the new ROVs. Among the buttons and toggle switches that confront the operator of one Phantom design is a control stick taken from a fighter jet aircraft. This device is the master, the robot arm—perhaps 1,000 feet distant—its slave. The forces from the operator-controlled stick are transmitted electronically to the underwater slave. Furthermore, when the slave makes contact with any object, it can be asked to report back the details. Electronic sensors on its claw gauge such qualities as hardness and texture, and send their findings to the surface computer. This translates them into a variety of acoustic tones: groaning sounds representing force, creaking for velocity and other characteristic sounds for tactile senses, which are so refined that they can even distinguish between a painted and an unpainted surface.

A wide range of space-age materials enhance the robots' toughness and versatility. Housings for lights, cameras, and sonar gear may be shaped from pressure-resistant ceramic compounds. Titanium frames are lighter than steel, and do not corrode in salt water. Kevlar fibers strengthen the signal cables.

Light, durable, tirelessly observant, the new ROVs have become the working class heroes of underwater endeavor. Engineers use them to inspect dams, locks, harbor facilities. Police forces send them down to retrieve lost objects and submerged evidence. Crab fishermen in the Bering Sea use them to monitor their traps; so clear are the images on the video screen that an operator can determine the sex of an individual crab. Maritime security agencies deploy ROVs in harbors to inspect ship hulls and guard against sabotage. One model, Phantom's *Watchdog*, sounds an underwater bullhorn to scare away intruders.

BRINGING UP THE TREASURE—REMOTELY

Shipwrecks on the sea floor—and there are untold thousands of them—offer not only the promise of occasional booty long since consigned to a watery grave; they also provide an insight into the customs and cultures of the past. But taking photographs or retrieving artifacts—especially from those wrecks that lie below scuba-diving range—proved virtually impossible until the advent of the remotely operated vehicle, or ROV, a robotic device that can be piloted by an operator sitting in a ship on the ocean's surface.

In order to retrieve an artifact or inspect a site—in this case a 4th-Century A.D. Roman shipwreck on the floor of the Mediterranean—the remotely operated vehicle *Jason* is lowered to the ocean floor from the research vessel *Star Hercules*. Instructions are relayed from the mother craft to its roving charge by a fiber-optic cable that transmits information in coded pulses of light.

An operator controls the ROV using a joystick; a television screen relays video images taken by a camera mounted on the robot *(inset at right)*. By manipulating the joystick, the operator can control thrusters that move it both horizontally and vertically. A separate joystick on the control board manipulates the ROV's mechanical hand. *Jason* has hoisted up 4-foot-long clay amphoras and yet its hand is delicate enough to pick up a teacup or a piece of coral.

Since ROVs can descend much deeper than divers—*Jason* can operate as deep as 20,000 feet—they have opened a new age in underwater archaeology. More than 90 percent of the ocean floor lies within their reach and humans need no longer risk their lives in their quest to reclaim the past.

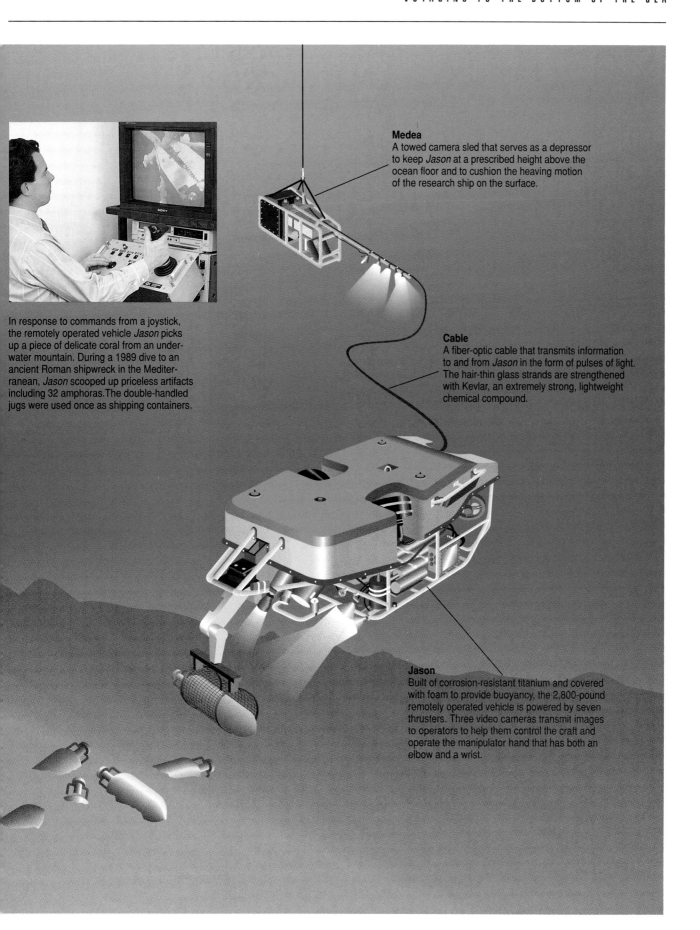

In response to commands from a joystick, the remotely operated vehicle *Jason* picks up a piece of delicate coral from an underwater mountain. During a 1989 dive to an ancient Roman shipwreck in the Mediterranean, *Jason* scooped up priceless artifacts including 32 amphoras. The double-handled jugs were used once as shipping containers.

Medea
A towed camera sled that serves as a depressor to keep *Jason* at a prescribed height above the ocean floor and to cushion the heaving motion of the research ship on the surface.

Cable
A fiber-optic cable that transmits information to and from *Jason* in the form of pulses of light. The hair-thin glass strands are strengthened with Kevlar, an extremely strong, lightweight chemical compound.

Jason
Built of corrosion-resistant titanium and covered with foam to provide buoyancy, the 2,800-pound remotely operated vehicle is powered by seven thrusters. Three video cameras transmit images to operators to help them control the craft and operate the manipulator hand that has both an elbow and a wrist.

Probing a Legend on the Ocean Floor

She slipped beneath the glassy-smooth surface of the North Atlantic Ocean on the night of April 14-15, 1912, the victim of a crushing collision with an iceberg. For 73 years the R.M.S. *Titanic*—once deemed unsinkable—lay unseen, entombed on the ocean floor, defying attempts to find her. In the early 1980s, millionaire Texan Jack Grimm—known as Cadillac Jack for his collection of vintage cars—financed three expeditions with the latest in sonar equipment but came up empty. Finally, on September 1, 1985, the *Titanic* was spotted by video cameras towed 2 1/2 miles below the water's surface by a research ship, directed by marine geologist Robert Ballard.

But while finding her represented one achievement, exploring the fabled wreck posed another challenge. The interlopers into this world of stygian darkness where the *Titanic* lay faced pressure of more than 6,000 pounds per square inch. Ballard decided to deploy an untried tagteam of the veteran submersible *Alvin* and a 210-pound remotely operated vehicle, *Jason Jr.*, or *JJ*.

The following summer Ballard descended 11 times to the Titanic in *Alvin*'s cramped 7-foot-sphere. During one dive, *Alvin* pilot Will Sellar settled the craft gently down on the ship's Boat Deck. Then, *JJ* pilot Martin Bowen took over. The 33-year-old marine biologist directed his charge out of a basket on the front of *Alvin*, controlling the robot's thrusters with a finger-sized joystick and a handgrip on a lap console. Tethered to its mother craft, *JJ* was able to move nimbly, neatly avoiding cables and obstructions that might have snared *Alvin*. Under Bowen's guidance, *JJ* probed the remains of the once-opulent Grand Staircase foyer, descending four stories inside the ship.

With a deep-towed camera sled, more than 53,000 photographs were taken, showing that the ship had been severed in two during its plunge to the ocean floor. No bodies were found; apparently, they had been consumed by organisms in the seawater. Neither was any sign seen of a suspected 250-foot-long gash on the starboard bow that many had postulated was inflicted by the iceberg. What *Alvin*'s passengers did observe were buckled hull plates. Instead of ripping the ship open like a can opener, the iceberg likely caused the riveted plates in the *Titanic*'s double-bottom hull to separate, allowing water to rush through the resulting cracks.

Steaming toward a fateful meeting with an iceberg on April 14, 1912, the 46,000-ton R.M.S. Titanic *was photographed only days before sinking on her maiden voyage, 350 miles off the coast of Newfoundland. More than 1,500 people went down with the ship.*

FINAL BERTH
In this painting by artist Ken Marschall, the Titanic *shows the effects of ploughing into the ocean floor at 30 miles per hour; the haunting image barely hints at the onetime opulence and grandeur of the ocean liner. The ship was ripped asunder during her plunge to the bottom and the two main pieces now lie half a mile apart on the ocean floor.*

The thousands of artifacts photographed from the Titanic wreck range from brass spittoons to champagne bottles. Here, a chandelier from the Grand Ballroom (left) and a rust-shrouded porthole (right) are captured by the roving eye of a camera mounted on the remotely operated vehicle Jason Jr.

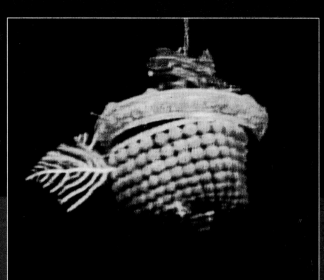

RESURRECTING THE PAST

Perhaps the most dramatic feats performed by ROVs are in the field of underwater archaeology. As many as 100,000 shipwrecks are believed to lie submerged in North American waters alone, dating from the time of Columbus to the present, and the toll from across the Atlantic echoes back into the fogbanks of antiquity. Many of these drowned vessels have long since broken up, their hulls wrenched apart by tides and currents, their timbers devoured by marine mollusks, their fittings rusted away or sheathed in coral. But a significant number have survived, at least in part. And each one represents a time capsule packed with clues as to the culture of its builders and the era of its demise. Many also represent a powerful enticement to treasure hunters. Ships have been the main carriers of the world's commerce and wealth from the time of the Pharaohs.

Often, the greatest challenge is to locate the wreck, especially in cases where no precise records exist of where the ship foundered. (The *Titanic* eluded discovery for years—even with sophisticated sonar devices—before she finally was located in 1985.) The process generally starts with a close scrutiny of shipping archives, in hopes of pinpointing the site of the disaster. Veteran diver Robert Stenuit is said to have labored 600 hours in various libraries before donning his scuba gear to discover the *Gerona*, a ship of the Spanish Armada lost off Ireland in 1588. Next comes a bottom survey of the suspected area—a task that may take months and cover hundreds of square miles. One problem is that most shipwrecks occur in shallow waters where the action of tides and currents soon breaks a vessel apart, or covers it with sand. Saltwater marine borers attack its timbers, leaving little but a coral-encrusted skeleton. The only clue to its whereabouts may be iron fittings or other ferrous artifacts, or the cargo itself, which is often scattered in a wide arc across the bottom. Hence metal detectors, or magnetometers, are frequently used.

Either handheld by a scuba diver, or towed above the bottom on a sled or ROV, a magnetometer picks up minute disturbances in the Earth's magnetic field that may indicate the presence of iron fastenings, anchors or cannon shot. An electronic version, known as the proton precession magnetometer, can detect a large steel hull from 180 yards, or an iron nail from about 10 feet.

For wider sweeps over a potential site, wreck hunters rely on sonar of various types. Side-scan sonar, in which the acoustic pulses beam outward from a torpedo-shaped towfish, can deliver a graphic image of the seafloor terrain 900 feet to either side (*page 86*). There is a tradeoff, however, between the range of the sweep and the sharpness of the picture. Beeps generated at low frequencies—30 kilohertz, say—penetrate farther, but show a fuzzy image. Higher frequencies of 50 to 500 kilohertz sacrifice distance for improved pictures. In either case, side-scan sonar shows only what rests on the bottom in plain view.

If a wreck has been covered by sand or sediment, its remnants still may be detected by a low-frequency sonar called a sub-bottom profiler. The pulses of sound, directed vertically, penetrate through sand and sediment until they strike bedrock. But anything in between, like a cannon or a chest full of ducats, shows up as a reflection on the sonar screen.

Not all sunken ships have disintegrated, and wrecks of more recent origin often reveal themselves visually. Such was the case with the *Titanic*—though it took Robert Ballard the full summer of 1985 to find it. His "eye" was a video camera mounted on a submersible sled called *Argo*, which he trailed across 140 square miles of ocean bottom. A few years later, in 1989, he used *Argo* again to locate the German battleship *Bismarck*, which plunged to the bottom in World War II taking most of its 2,200-man crew to a watery grave.

Video detection has one striking drawback, however: the limited visibility in most submarine environments. To counteract the problem, underwater archaeologists can use a computer-age system to improve existing images. Called histogram equalization, the process begins with the use of a semiconducting silicon chip in an electronic still camera called a Charge Coupled Device. The postage-stamp-size device records the electrical charge that accumulates when light strikes the surface of an object. By measuring the charge that builds up in each section of the chip—called a picture element, or pixel—it is possible to estimate accurately the amount of light striking there. Each pixel—a single photo may contain several million picture elements—is given a numerical value that corresponds to a grayness scale. Simple CCDs might register 256 levels, 0 being black and 255 being pure white. Very advanced CCDs can record more than 32,000 levels. The range depends on how many bits are used. A bit is a single digit of binary code—a 0 or 1—and is the basic unit of computer information. Eight bits—or one byte—can create any number between 0 and 256; to create a greater range, more bits are required. An eight-bit CCD will record 256 grayness levels, but for any one picture most values for pixels would likely fall in the middle range between, say, 80 and 160. With histogram equalization, scientists take those values and "stretch" them over the 256 range, which provides even finer resolution. Now, that same range of pixel values is reconfigured to fit a range from 0 to 255.

Another solution to the problem of murky underwater images may be a scanning laser device, encased in a two-foot-long tube that is towed near the ocean floor. A narrow beam of very bright blue-green light is projected through an oscillating mirror at one end of the device; its return signal then is detected by one of a series of diodes mounted near the other end of the tube. By knowing the angle at which the beam is projected and the angle at which it is received, plus the distance between the mirror and the specific diode, the distance to each of the objects at a wreck can be determined by geometry. Each time the laser completes a scan a contour is generated. With thousands of measurements produced by the laser, a computer can create a precise three-dimensional view of a site. Blue-green is the color usually used because it has the lowest level of light absorption in water. (This also accounts for the fact that the ocean appears blue.)

Finding and viewing an underwater archaeological site is one thing; recording precisely the placement of each object is another. In the past, the mapping was usually accomplished by dividing the site into a grid pattern, and applying a tape measure to pinpoint each item, in much the same way that archaeologists work on land. But divers can now rely on an acoustical method called SHARPS—or Sonic High-Accuracy Ranging and Positioning System. Three sound-emitting devices called transducers are dropped to mark the site. The diver carries a fourth transducer, which can be beamed at any particular object. A surface receiver registers the beeps and records the position *(page 132)*.

Once a wrecked vessel is located, and its contents sorted out, the problem becomes how to retrieve the booty. If the artifacts lie in shallow water they can

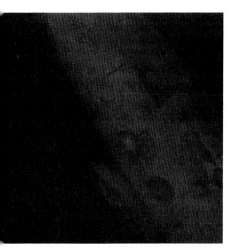

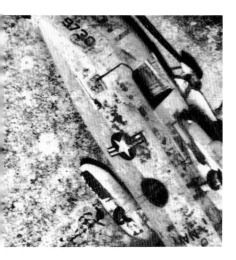

These two photographs of a U.S. Navy helicopter that lies in 3,300 feet of water off the coast of the Bahamas demonstrate the power of the histogram equalization process to enhance an existing photograph of an object underwater. The original photo of the helicopter taken by an electronic still camera (top) *was murky and difficult to decipher. By using a computer program that refines the gray scale, the helicopter was revealed—insignia and all* (bottom).

MAPPING WITH SOUND

Once an archaeological site is found, it has to be mapped to record each artifact's relative position. In the past, moving underwater with a tape measure in hand proved to be a laborious process. But SHARPS—or Sonic High Accuracy Ranging and Positioning System—an acoustically generated grid system, allows a diver or a remotely operated vehicle (ROV) to map an underwater site quickly and accurately in three dimensions.

From a research boat, three transceivers that can emit and receive high-frequency acoustic signals are dropped to the floor in a triangular formation around the area to be mapped. A fourth, mobile transceiver is held by a diver who triggers the unit while tracing site objects. As each object is traced, the gun emits acoustic signals, which are received by the fixed transceivers. They, in turn, transmit their signals by cable to a SHARPS-programmed computer shipside, which can record up to 10 measurements a second. By measuring the travel time of the acoustic pulses to each fixed transceiver, the computer can—by triangulation—track the diver's hand as an accurate picture of the site is drawn. And by knowing the depth of the mobile transceiver, scientists also can create a real-time, three-dimensional view on the computer monitor.

Because SHARPS works with sound and not light, it is not affected by murky water; accuracy is better than one-half inch. A three-dimensional record of a shipwreck that once would have taken weeks can now be done in a matter of hours with little disturbance to the site.

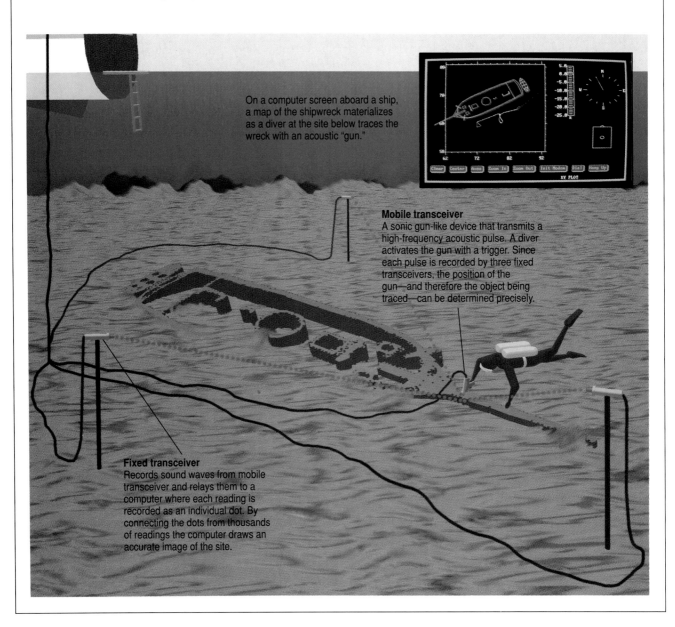

On a computer screen aboard a ship, a map of the shipwreck materializes as a diver at the site below traces the wreck with an acoustic "gun."

Mobile transceiver
A sonic gun-like device that transmits a high-frequency acoustic pulse. A diver activates the gun with a trigger. Since each pulse is recorded by three fixed transceivers, the position of the gun—and therefore the object being traced—can be determined precisely.

Fixed transceiver
Records sound waves from mobile transceiver and relays them to a computer where each reading is recorded as an individual dot. By connecting the dots from thousands of readings the computer draws an accurate image of the site.

To collect gold coins en masse from the Central America, which sank 200 miles off Charleston, South Carolina, in 1854, salvagers cover the coins with a silicone compound, sprayed from a hose into a metal box that is lowered to the ocean floor. The substance hardens into a congealed mat, which can then be picked up with the coins safely embedded inside.

be brought up by divers. But with a deep wreck—one that lies thousands of feet down—the problem is much greater.

Such is the case with the *Central America*, a 300-foot paddlewheel steamer that sank in 1857 while carrying 580 passengers and a hoard of California gold from Panama to New York. Her whereabouts remained a mystery until 1988, when deep-sea mining engineer Thomas Thompson discovered the ship off South Carolina in 8,000 feet of water. Thompson and his crew surveyed the area with side-scan sonar, spending 40 days to sweep 1,400 square miles. Then he sent down his custom-built ROV, *Nemo*, for a closer look. Now *Nemo* is bringing up the gold using a process known as silicone injection. To pick up piles of coins at a time, *Nemo* lowers a two-foot-square open-ended box around the coins. A silicone base and a rubber catalyst—both stored in separate tanks on *Nemo*—are pumped in through the top. The compound flows over the coins and then hardens within five hours. The whole block is lifted onto a special tray that fits inside the ROV. Back on board the mother ship, the crew removes the silicone block, slices it open and removes the coins without destroying the impression they leave. The block then is used to provide a record of how the coins were found *in situ*. Coins scattered over the site are retrieved individually by *Nemo* with tiny suction-cup fingers.

Using *Nemo*'s two manipulator arms, the *Central America*'s salvagers have hauled up walnut-sized nuggets from the California gold rush, along with gold dust and gold bars—one weighing more than 60 pounds. It is a bonanza for Thompson and his investors, and also for the museums, coin collectors and historians.

The payoffs extend far beyond such immediate financial rewards. When the ROV *Jason* dived to an ancient Roman shipwreck in the Mediterranean in May 1989, video images were transmitted by satellite and relayed to educational institutions and museums around North America. More than 200,000 students watched and marveled as *Jason* gently picked up artifacts from the sea floor. It was the first live broadcast of its kind ever attempted from the deep sea. The following year, 60 students were able to take command of the ROV during another live underwater broadcast. As the young explorers manipulated the joystick controls at their schools, the messages were transmitted by satellite and fiber-optic cable to *Jason* during a dive to the wrecks of two U.S. warships that sank in the War of 1812.

Both events were part of the Jason Project, spearheaded by *Titanic* discoverer Robert Ballard to stimulate an interest in science among young students. By bringing the underwater world directly into the lives of the next generation of oceanographers and marine archaeologists, the Jason Project may sow the seeds of technology that will retrieve a past that even now—with a growing armada of robots and submersibles scouring the ocean floor—lies largely untouched and undetected. And that could be the richest treasure of all.

The Oceans and Global Warming

When scientists in the 1960s detected that the Earth might be warming, their quest for causes drew them to the oceans. Small wonder. The oceans cover more than two-thirds of the Earth, and, like a giant thermostat, help regulate global climate. Ocean currents transport heat to cold regions such as the poles, keeping them from freezing over completely; they also convey cold water to the Equator, cooling the Earth in the tropical regions. Moreover, the oceans absorb several billion tons of carbon dioxide yearly from the atmosphere. Unchecked, a buildup of this gas helps trap solar heat re-emitted from the Earth as infrared radiation. The result of this phenomenon, called the greenhouse effect, eventually may produce a gradual warming of global temperatures.

The speed at which global warming is occurring—and even whether it is occurring at all—are issues still being debated. Fossil-fuel emissions—from car exhausts and industries—have increased the amount of carbon dioxide in the atmosphere, exceeding the ocean's ability to consume it. Some scientists believe that those heat-trapping gases have raised temperatures worldwide in the last century; others argue that any changes could well be part of long-term fluctuations in climate that have produced recurrent Ice Ages and tropical conditions worldwide throughout Earth's history.

If global warming is occurring, certain results can be inferred. One is a rise in sea level. A warming of even several degrees would cause a minute fraction of the polar ice sheets to melt and the sea level to rise. The result could be enormously disruptive—and not just to shoreline communities. By altering a major ocean current called the Oceanic Conveyor Belt, melting might affect global weather patterns. The conveyor runs from the polar regions along the ocean floor to the Equator where it mixes with warm water and rises to the surface and returns to the poles. As the melting glaciers dilute the surface water in the extreme latitudes with their less-dense, less-saline water, the conveyor—which is driven by the sinking of salt-rich waters in the polar regions—may slow down. If the conveyor stops, the transport of cold water to the Equator and warm water to the poles will cease. In a few hundred years, the poles might start to freeze over and the tropics could become unbearably hot.

To counteract this warming trend, some have suggested stocking the oceans with more gas-absorbing phytoplankton, the microscopic algae that support life in the oceans. Most of the oceans' CO_2 intake is used as an ingredient for plankton's photosynthesis. The feasibility of raising plankton on enormous "farms" or adding chemicals to Antarctic waters to spawn planktonic growth there are being studied and these ideas may eventually help to subtract the carbon dioxide overload from the atmosphere.

But many scientists fear that tampering with nature is dangerous. They say that until oceanographers fully understand how the ocean works, it is safer to cut gas emissions than to manipulate oceans to counteract their effects. By intervening, mankind may create more problems than it solves.

If global warming is occurring, as many scientists suspect, the melting of ice in the polar regions—such as this glacier in Alaska—could threaten a climate-regulating conveyor belt current that flows through the world's oceans.

Cleaning Up

When the supertanker *Exxon Valdez*, laden with more than 53 million gallons of oil, ran aground on Bligh Reef off the coast of Alaska in 1989, 11 million gallons gushed through its torn hull into the Pacific before the leak was stanched. Disastrous though it was, the spill was but a tincture compared to the more than half-billion gallons of oil that enter the oceans annually. Oil has been seeping into the ocean from subsurface reservoirs and the erosion of oil-saturated soils for at least 100,000 years. Still, the most intense pollution has occurred in the last 100 years. Spills are the most notorious oil problem because of their immediate visibility, but modern cities inconspicuously dump and drain far greater amounts of oil, sewage and toxins into the oceans every day.

With time–sometimes many years— the ocean can purify itself of oil spills, geological seepage and toxic chemicals. Some of the pollutants evaporate; some wash ashore; some are consumed by bacteria and other microorganisms. Still, while the effects of toxic wastes are not fully understood, one thing is certain: In the short term, the effects on the ocean's ecosystems can be far-reaching. Pollutants can be transformed by water, light and marine organisms, sometimes triggering blooms of toxic algae more potent than the original toxin. Birds and fish then transport the toxins to other parts of the world; the cycle is completed when humans consume the foods tainted by their own industry.

Oil industries are working to devise better ways to clean up their spills. Floating booms, skimming devices and absorbant belts do slowly mop up spillage. Spraying oil with a chemical dispersant to speed its break-up for organic consumption is another technique. The success of these and other measures, however, often depends on unreliable factors such as calm waters or immediate large-scale action. And even when successful, the oil cleaned is minimal next to the widespread problems. But here, too, help may be on the way. Since 1972, when a United Nations conference on the environment was held in Stockholm, Sweden, there have been substantial efforts to reduce pollution in the ocean. And in 1983, a global moratorium on radioactive waste dumping was imposed.

But little is being done to stave off the greatest threat to the seas: land-based pollution. Run-off into coastal waters, pipeline discharge and carbon emissions from the air make up at least 80 percent of the problem. Oceanographers say it is still not too late to clean up the oceans. Not yet, anyway.

To push oil from the Exxon Valdez *spill back to the water's edge where it could be collected better, workers on Green Island, Alaska, used high-pressure hoses. But the method may have had unexpected effects: Some scientists now think the process may have killed many of the organisms on the coast that had survived the spill.*

A Question of Survival

The human imagination would be hard pressed to have invented a mightier mammal than the whale. To witness a 100-foot long, 100-ton blue whale rising majestically from the depths is a sublime experience—and one that has become increasingly rare in the 20th Century. By the 1960s, the blue whale, and other large cetaceans, such as the humpback and fin whale, had been hunted by man so thoroughly that they were about to follow the dinosaur into extinction.

But in 1972 the trend was disrupted when activists from Greenpeace began setting up human barricades, placing small boats between the hunters and the hunted. Their "Save the Whale" campaign did more than capture world-wide public sympathy for whales; it served as a focus for concern over all endangered species and for the environment at large.

Public pressure to ban commercial whaling came to fruition in steps. Moratoriums were put into effect, first on the hunting of whales thought to be most endangered, and then, in 1982, on the hunting of all whales for an indefinite period beginning in 1986. Proposed by the International Whaling Commission (IWC), which was established in 1946 to set limits on the number of whales killed per year, the 1986 moratorium was a means to regenerate whale populations for future hunting, which then would be controlled strictly to protect the whale.

A few countries, including Japan and Iceland, continue to hunt whales, ignoring or circumventing the moratorium. Still, most whaling nations respect the ban and some whales, such as the eastern Pacific gray, are

returning to
the oceans in encouraging numbers.
Others, though, such as the North Atlantic
right whale, are having trouble rebounding
despite strict conservation measures of many
years. Scientists are at a loss to explain exactly why some species have fared better than
others. Theories suggest that there may not
be enough food to sustain all whale populations, or that inbreeding among some
species has weakened their genetic lines,
decreasing their survival rates. Ocean pollution is another suspect in the mystery. Marine
biologists find it hard to count whales and are

reluctant to
estimate their numbers; scientific over-esti-
mates in the past have encouraged whalers
to hunt several species almost to the brink of
extinction without realizing it. The commission has the power to lift or partially lift the
moratorium at any time. Until more is known
about the number of whales and their reproductive habits, some scientists hope that, at
the very least, the present global moratorium
will be sustained.

*Some species of whales—such as these
two humpbacks—have increased their stock
in recent decades. Some smaller species,
however, are closer now to extinction
than they ever have been.*

Index

Numerals in *italics* indicate an illustration of the subject mentioned.

PICTURE CREDITS

ILLUSTRATION CREDITS

ACKNOWLEDGMENTS

The editors wish to thank the following:
Roger Anderson, Schilling Development Inc., Davis, CA; Jim M. Barrett, Deputy Director, AT&T Submarine Systems, Inc., Morristown, NJ; Andy Bowen, Woods Hole Oceanographic Institution, Woods Hole, MA; Bruce Cornuelle, Scripps Institution of Oceanography, La Jolla, CA; Ed DiCastro, Emerson & Cuming Inc., Canton, MA; David Eaton, DCIEM, Downsview, Ont.; Robert Evans, Columbus-America Discovery Group, Columbus, OH; John W. Farrington, Associate Director of Education and Dean of Graduate Studies, Woods Hole Oceanographic Institution, Woods Hole, MA; Andrew Fisher, Ocean Drilling Program, Texas A&M University, College Station, TX; Frank Geisel, Marquest Group Inc., Bourne, MA; Robert Gerard, Lamont-Doherty Geological Observatory, Palisades, NY; Dr. Frank Gonzalez, NOAA-PMEL, Seattle, WA; Prof. Samuel H. Gruber, Director of Bimini Biological Field Station, Universtity of Miami, Miami, FL; Christopher Harrold, Monterey Bay Aquarium, Monterey, CA; Gene Hemsworth, Professional Association of Diving Instructors (Canada), Sydney, B.C.; Ted Hess, Oceaneering International, Morgan City, LA; Dr. Robert Hessler, Scripps Institution of Oceanography, La Jolla, CA; Dr. Johannes Kylstra, Durham, NC; Tom LaPuzza, Public Affairs Officer, Naval Oceans Systems Center, San Diego, CA; Gayle Laurin, Sierra Geophysics Inc., Kirkland, WA; David M. Lavigne, Department of Zoology, University of Guelph, Guelph, ONT.; Shelly Lauzon, Woods Hole Oceanographic Institution, Woods Hole, MA; Pat Linley, Public Affairs, Harbor Branch Oceanographic Institution, Fort Pierce, FL; George Milkowski, University of Rhode Island Graduate School of Oceanography, RI; Elizabeth Miller, Deep Ocean Engineering Inc., San Leandro, CA; Scott Morrison, International Hard Suits, North Vancouver, B.C.; National Oceanic and Atmospheric Administration, Rockville, MD; Catherine Offinger, Marquest Group Inc., Bourne, MA; Dan Orr, Divers Alert Network, Durham, NC; Leo E. Overhiser, Senior Engineer, AT&T Submarine Systems, Inc., Morristown, NJ; Kevin M. Reeds, Trimble Navigation Ltd., Sunnyvale, CA; Karen Riedel, Ocean Drilling Program, Texas A&M University, College Station, TX; Dayna M. Risebrow, Trimble Navigation Ltd., Sunnyvale, CA; William B.F. Ryan, Lamont-Doherty Geological Observatory, Palisades, NY; Public Affairs Office, Scripps Institution of Oceanography, La Jolla, CA; Susan R. Spies, Public Affairs, AT&T Submarine Systems, Inc., Morristown, NJ; Ken Stewart, Woods Hole Oceanographic Institution, Woods Hole, MA; Michael A. Storms, Ocean Drilling Program, Texas A&M University, College Station, TX; Sue Threshie, Monterey Bay Aquarium, Monterey, CA; Alexandra Tolstoy, Naval Research Laboratory, Washington, D.C.; Barrie B. Walden, Woods Hole Oceanographic Institution, Woods Hole, MA; Don Wilke, Scripps Institution of Oceanography, La Jolla, CA; Dana Yoerger, Woods Hole Oceanographic Institution, Woods Hole, MA.

The following persons also assisted in the preparation of this book:
Megan Durnford, Jenny Meltzer, Shirley Sylvain and Hugh Wilson.

This book was designed on Apple Macintosh® computers, using QuarkXPress® in conjunction with CopyFlow™ and a Linotronic® 300R for page layout and composition; StrataVision 3d®, Adobe Illustrator 88® and Adobe Photoshop® were used as illustration programs.